# The Natural Breakfast Book

by the Editors of Rodale Press
compiled and prepared by Carol Stoner

Rodale Press, Inc./ Book Division / Emmaus, Pa. 18049

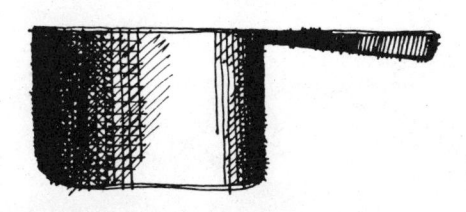

Designed by John K. Landis

ISBN 0-87857-063-2

Library of Congress Catalogue No. 72-93740

COPYRIGHT 1973 by RODALE PRESS, INC.

All rights reserved. No part of this publication may be reproduced or transmitted in any form or by any means, electronic or mechanical, including photocopy, recording, or any information storage and retrieval system.

ORGANIC LIVING PAPERBACKS are published by
Rodale Press, Inc., Book Division
Emmaus, Pennsylvania 18049

JB-7

FIRST PRINTING   May, 1973

PRINTED IN THE U.S.A.
on recycled paper

# Contents

|   | Introduction | 1 |
|---|---|---|
| Chapter 1. | Natural Cereals from Whole Grains | 5 |
| 2. | The Art of Making Bread | 27 |
| 3. | Butter, Nut and Fruit Spreads | 38 |
| 4. | Corn Meal: An Early American Staple | 49 |
| 5. | Eggs: The Most Nearly-Perfect Protein Food | 58 |
| 6. | Protein for Breakfast with Meat, Fish and Cheese | 71 |
| 7. | Sugar—Thirty-two Empty Calories per Teaspoon | 91 |
| 8. | Honey—The Natural Sweetener | 94 |
| 9. | Pancakes, Waffles and French Toast Made More Nourishing | 98 |
| 10. | "Grow Your Own" Yogurt | 104 |
| 11. | Fruits and Fruit Juices | 112 |
| 12. | Herb Teas | 120 |
| 13. | Convenient Breakfast Foods for Hurried Mornings | 123 |
| 14. | Breakfasts for People Who Hate Breakfasts | 127 |
| 15. | Breakfasts Are a Must, Diet or No Diet | 134 |
|   | Index | 138 |

# Introduction

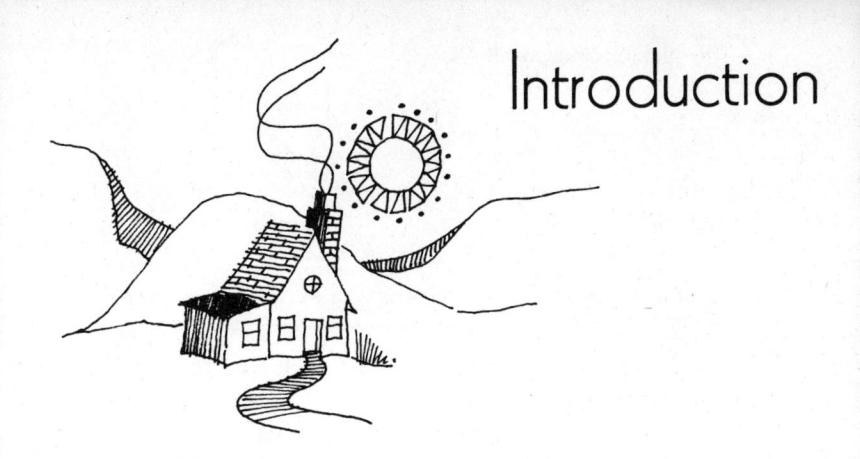

Can you remember a *real* breakfast—a breakfast before the days of sugar-coated cereal, jam-filled toaster snacks and breakfast-in-a-packet? I'm thinking of a breakfast like the one Thomas Wolfe wrote about in *Look Homeward, Angel*:

> "In the morning, they rose in a house pungent with breakfast cookery, and they sat at a smoking table loaded with brains and eggs, ham, hot biscuits, fried apples seething in their gummed syrups, honey, golden butter, fried steaks, scalding coffee. Or there were stacked batter-cakes, rum-colored molasses, fragrant brown sausages, a bowl of wet cherries, plums, fat juicy bacon, jam."

Now, that's a real breakfast.

I can remember *my* breakfasts, all right, but the memory isn't necessarily one that I cherish. When I was a child, I abhorred the traditional breakfast foods. I wouldn't touch an egg, a bowl of cereal or a piece of toast. But I *was* hungry in the morning, so I'd open the refrigerator and search until I found something that appealed to me—maybe a piece of meat loaf or some left-over spaghetti. But my favorite breakfast was a salami sandwich on white bread—washed down with a Pepsi! My mother didn't like this at all but figured that it was better than nothing, so she let me get away with eating like that.

My reaction to breakfast was not so strange. Breakfast has become a pretty unexciting meal. We don't take time for the kind of breakfasts that Wolfe wrote about. What we do eat is dull and tasteless: supermarket-storage eggs, plastic bread, crinkled cereals. But why bother with preparing all that? Breakfast now comes conveniently packaged for us in little aluminum foil envelopes: just tear open, then stir the contents into milk (skim milk, at that).

In contrast, consider the life style of my friend, Jennifer Ann Voehringer. Jenny is the two-year-old daughter of a neighboring organic farmer. Her breakfast eggs come straight from the family chickens—gathered by her father just before breakfast. The milk she drinks for breakfast is from the neighbor's cow—so is the butter which Jenny's mother makes in their blender from the skimmed-off cream. The honey that Jenny loves on her home-baked bread comes from the family's beehives. The apples and pears that Jenny gobbles so readily are from trees growing in one of their family's pastures. Her cereal, granola, is homemade from organically-grown grains and is topped with fresh fruit and milk. Jenny has never known a breakfast of sugar-coated cereal.

My husband and I are not so fortunate as Jenny and her family. We don't raise much of our own food—not yet, anyway. But we hardly ever eat any food that has been handled by a food processor or a supermarket. Most of it is organically-grown, a lot comes straight from farmers we know.

When we started to get turned off by the tastelessness of mass-produced food, we began to look for places where we could buy natural, organically-raised food that still had some original flavor and texture. There are eight natural food stores within 25 miles of our home, and we began our search in these. One of these stores has its own grain mill. Now we can get any organically-grown grain, stone ground to order, at a price cheaper per pound than pre-packaged organic flour.

We buy unrefined oils from another natural food store that sells a good variety of oils stored in large, spouted crocks. If we bring our own bottles, we can save up to a quarter of the price of pre-bottled oils. And these oils resemble the foods from which they are derived because they have not been refined and bleached to a sterile clarity. The corn germ oil really tastes like sweet corn and has its color; the oilve oil smells of olives, and the sesame oil is just as light and delicate in flavor as its seeds.

The same store also sells everything we need for our homemade breakfast cereals. We buy oatmeal, nuts, seeds, grain flakes and dried fruit by the pound, scooped from big barrels.

These natural food stores could supply us with most of the things we needed, but since we wanted to make some connections with the actual growers of the food we ate, we asked around for the names of organic farms within a reasonable driving distance of our home. The natural-food-store people were helpful, and so were the natural mineral-fertilizer dealers and the people at the farm supply stores. Thanks to them, we now get organically-raised beef from a farm 30 miles away. The grower sells only by the half steer, but we had little trouble finding a friend who wanted to share a side of beef with us. The 120 pounds or so that we buy at one time will last the two of us for six months.

We learned of another farmer in the area, who sells organically-raised pork so tender and lean that regular customers find it best to call a few months before butchering time to place their orders.

Our county agent gave us the name of another organic farmer who has fruits and vegetables to sell in season, and our State Department of Agriculture sent us a list of dairies in the state who have certified herds and are permitted by law to sell raw milk. An ad in the local newspaper helped us to locate a woman who now sells us weekly three dozen big eggs from free-ranging hens fed organically-grown grains. Through the local beekeepers' society we found a man who sells both buckwheat and clover honey that are uncooked and unfiltered. We buy natural cheeses cut from huge rounds at a family-owned-and-operated stand at our local farmers' market.

Our shopping trips are a little longer and more involved but far more interesting than the supermarket circuit we used to follow. We've learned a lot about how food is grown and a lot about nutrition. We've met many fine people and have even made some new friends. We've grown to appreciate good food, and last, but not least, we're having much better breakfasts.

Obviously, not every family can have its own organic farm, but we all have access to organically-grown—or at least unprocessed—foods. There's no real reason for any family to put up with the "American breakfast syndrome" for even one more morning!

*Carol Stoner*

# Natural Cereals from Whole Grains

When it comes to food value, nearly all of today's breakfast cereals are as nutritious as a candy bar. Cold, processed cereal (the kind most American children eat for breakfast) is one of the worst foods with which to begin the day. Ads tell us that commercial breakfast cereals are loaded with food value, when in reality those snazzy cereal boxes are filled with over-processed, lifeless grains. Many of them depend on sugar to mask their tastelessness. Very few come close to being the body-building foods the TV commercials say they are.

Consider corn flakes, the most popular dry cereal and one of the least adulterated of all the commercial cereals. Here is how it's made:

The kernels of corn, fairly rich in protein, phosphorus, three B vitamins and vitamin A, are plunged into a lye bath, then cooked in live steam. This puts quite a strain on the nutritional value of the finished product. Then the corn kernels are mixed with a flavoring syrup heavy with refined sugar. They are dried and rolled under 75 tons of pressure by rollers hot with friction, toasted in an oven, and, finally, shucked into a brightly colored box with an impressive list of nutrients printed on the outside.

What is left of the vitamin A that was in the original kernels is miniscule. The known B vitamins have been stamped out so thoroughly by cooking and heating that the manufacturers feel constrained to add synthetic imitations. Any protein that might have survived this mechanical mauling is so transformed that it is probably useless.

When breakfast cereals are of the best quality, they are nutritionally equivalent to whole grain bread. The usual over-processed and sugared sort are more nearly equivalent to a starchy dessert, which few informed people would consider a satisfactory breakfast food.

The only real nutrition to be had from eating dry cereals such as this comes from the milk customarily poured over them. Yet, decades of tradition, and some 80 million dollars spent annually in advertising, have conditioned the American public to regard ready-to-eat breakfast cereals as the last word in morning nourishment. Because children are especially susceptible to advertising, they are the chief targets of promotional campaigns for cereals. Thirty to forty percent of the ad dollars are directed at the kids. Just take a stroll down the cereal aisle of a supermarket and count the cereal boxes that attempt to seduce children with games, trinkets and other gimmicks. The December 1967 issue of *Fortune,* in an article entitled, "The Fight for a Place at the Breakfast Table," says that there were 66 brands of cereal distributed in that year and that about 25 of them had been introduced since 1965. Imagine how that number has grown by now!

Most of today's dry cereals, especially those made for children, whether "fortified" or not, consist largely of sugar. Robert B. Choate, "citizen lobbyist," No. 1 enemy of commercial cereal companies, and chairman of the Council on Children, Media and Merchandising, did a study of the sugar content of 25 popular cereals in 1970—and discovered that they contained from 35 to 51 percent refined sugar. "Our children," he concluded, "are being programmed to demand sugar and sweeteners in every food." Of 60 cereals studied by Choate for nutritional qualities, 40 brands were rated as nutritionally inadequate, because, according to Choate, they provide "empty calories and little else."

Testifying before the Senate Consumer Subcommittee, Joan Gussow, a leader of a study done by nutritionists and students at Columbia University said that children are barraged with TV commercials that are "blatantly anti-nutritional." She said that the intention of the study was to pick out misleading commercials, but they found that "the whole was considerably worse than the sum of its parts." Her conclusion was that "cereals, as described on children's television, are oversweetened, overpriced and overpromoted."

In another attack on boxed cereals, former Nader Raider, Michael J. Jacobson accused cereal companies of wooing children with hazardous food colorings. In a 1972 testimony before the Senate's Consumer Subcommittee, Jacobson said that Americans ingested 105,881 pounds of artificial coloring in their breakfast cereal during the first five months of 1967, "and undoubtedly the figure is much higher today." He called the use of synthetic coloring in cereals "an obvious example whereby chemicals introduce a health hazard without contributing any real benefit."

The anti-oxident preservatives, BHT and BHA have also come under fire from Mr. Jacobson. BHT and BHA have been subjected to only the most rudimentary cancer tests, Jacobson claimed. "To what extent they increase shelf life of breakfast cereals I do not know," he said. "But I would prefer that delivery trucks make more frequent visits to grocery stores than have poorly-tested BHT and BHA accumulate in my body."

Of course you'll hardly find a modern breakfast cereal on the market now that isn't "fortified" with synthetic minerals and vitamins. But that is because the processing has removed most of the nutrients that were present originally. Those intended to "fortify" are usually added in quantities so minute as to be almost useless. Why not just refine the cereal grains enough to make them marketable but still leave much of the original food value intact? It would certainly mean less processing, less "fortification." The end product would be natural food value in a whole, more satisfying cereal.

In their natural states, grains are some of the most economical foods available. Adding on the cost of the little processing really necessary to make these foods marketable, the cereals would still be inexpensive. Oatmeals, cream of wheat, cream of oats and buckwheat cereals are priced at about 30 cents a pound. Organically-grown grains are about the same. But if a food factory gets hold of the natural grains and turns them into a sugary-sweet product, the price jumps to two and three times the price of the natural wholesome cereals.

Not all dry, cold cereals are nutritionally worthless—just most of them. If you look carefully

## Natural Cereals from Whole Grains

There is no need to rely on commercially-made natural cereals, since they are so easy to make at home. Mix up large quantities at a time. You can serve them during the morning rush hour just as quickly as you can pour a sugary commercial cereal out of its box. Once you've got the cereal made, keep it in a tightly-sealed jar under refrigeration. For longer storage, freeze it.

Rolled oats is the basic ingredient. Add whatever else you like—raisins, rye and wheat flakes, dried apricots, dates, apples, peaches, pears or bananas, buckwheat groats, corn meal, sesame and sunflower seeds, whole grain flours, coconut, sliced almonds, chopped nuts, wheat germ, honey, maple syrup or date sugar, and pure vanilla extract and sea salt for flavoring.

A recipe really isn't necessary, but if this is new to you and you would feel more confident using a tested recipe, use one from a natural foods cookbook, or try one of these adaptations:

3 parts rolled oats
1 part sesame seeds
1 part sunflower seeds
1 part sliced almonds
1 part shredded, unsweetened coconut
½ part wheat germ
½ part soya flour
1 part corn meal
¼ part unrefined oil
½ part uncooked, unfiltered honey
—hot water
1 part raisins

Mix together all the dry ingredients except the raisins. Add just enough hot water to the oil and honey to dissolve them. Mix the liquids into the dry combination. Add more water until the dry mixture is moist. Spread on a cookie sheet and toast lightly in a 325°F oven. Add raisins. Serve with milk or apple juice.

For an untoasted, Swiss-type cereal, mix together:

3 parts rolled oats
1 part dried date pieces
1 part raisins
1 part chopped nuts
1 part rye flakes
1 part sunflower seeds
1 part sesame seeds

Serve with milk or juice.

Don't go halfway when you make your own cereal; shop carefully for quality ingredients. There are excellent sources available if you take the time and effort to read labels and ask questions.

Cereal grains are the primary sources of nourishment for millions of people around the world. These people, many of whom seldom eat meat, get much of their protein, vitamins and minerals from unrefined grains. Grains are the most popular item in the organic food market right now. People who won't settle for commercially-grown and processed grains are relying on organic growers to provide wholesome grains—free from chemicals and over-refining.

If you are unfamiliar with whole grains, here are some of the basic ones you should have in your cupboard:

# Rice

About 90 percent of the world's rice is grown in the hot, wet lands of Asia, extending from India to Japan. This grain is consumed daily by people in that part of the world. Because money and technology are limited in these nations, must rural Asians do the reaping, threshing and milling by hand. They remove only the husk, leaving the grain intact. This is natural brown rice. In this form it contains the protein, starch, fat, minerals and vitamins with which it was first endowed. White rice, the kind commonly found in this country, is a highly-processed grain that has had most of the nutrients removed merely for aesthetic appeal and good keeping qualities. In the last few years, however, brown rice has found its place in our markets, thanks to health-conscious retailers and consumers.

Most brown rice, especially that in natural food stores, is organically-grown. It is fortunate that organically-grown brown rice is easily found in stores because chemically-grown rice is one of the most heavily sprayed crops. The paddies where it is grown are sprayed with Parathion (which has the highest toxicity rating of all chemicals) or Barbaryl (Sevin), or the soil is treated with copper sulfate to kill off tadpole shrimp that endanger the seedlings. The seeds themselves are also doused with chemical insecticides, pesticides, herbicides and chemical fertilizers.

Brown rice comes in long grain and short grain varities. Short grain rice takes less time to cook and contains slightly less protein than the longer grain variety. Rice grits, coarsely-ground grains of brown rice, are popular as quick-cooking hot cereals, and rice flakes make a nutritous cold cereal. Rice cream is a powdered form of natural brown rice that makes good cream of rice for breakfast. If rice cream is not available in your area you can easily make your own. Here's a quick, easy recipe using organic brown rice.

## Cream of Brown Rice

Wash 2 cups of brown rice in cold water. Drain well. Cook in a dry skillet about 5 minutes until rice is completely dry. Grind to a powder at high speed in an electric blender or several times in a home grain mill. Return rice to pan and toast lightly. Store in a tightly covered jar. Prepare as you would cream of rice.

## Millet

In northern China as well as in much of Africa and India, millet, not rice, is the staple grain. The natives steam the millet to form a porridge. Sometimes it is coarsely-ground into flour for puddings and flat cakes. Millet seeds vary greatly in size, shape and color, but those commonly available in this country are tiny, shiny-white or cream-colored ovals. Millet is a particularly nutritious grain containing large amounts of magnesium and potassium.

Cracked millet has a finer texture than the

pearl-like grains and cooks quicker. Millet may be cracked in a home blender or grain mill. The cooked grain is tender, yet chewy, and is ideal for puddings and cereals. Both millet flakes and puffed millet are available at natural food stores and by mail-order from Walnut Acres, Penn's Creek, Pennsylvania 17862.

# Barley

A popular food in North Africa and in parts of Europe, barley has been found among the ruins of the oldest known structures built by man. The crop is very hardy, growing even within the Arctic Circle.

Most of us are familiar with the "pearled" variety of barley, popularized in Scotch broth and soups. The bran has been removed and the grain polished. Where barley is considered a mainstay in the diet, however, "naked barley" is used. In this type, the grain is left loosely surrounded by the husks in the threshing. Barley, like rice, contributes significant amounts of calcium to the diet.

# Buckwheat

Buckwheat, often called groats or kasha, is not actually a member of the grass family. It is related to rhubarb and sorrel but is cultivated and consumed in much the same way as cereal grains. Although one of the least important crops in America, it is one of the most popular foods in Russia.

Buckwheat contains 11 to 15 percent good quality protein—even more than corn. In terms of protein actually absorbed by the body, buckwheat excels rye, whole wheat and soybean flours. It is a fine source of the B vitamins, especially thiamin and riboflavin. The Department of Agriculture Home Economics Report No. 36 points out that dark buckwheat flour is exceptionally rich in vitamins $B_6$ and pantothenic acid. Actually, it has three times the vitamin $B_6$ and pantothenic acid of whole wheat flour and is a good source of copper, manganese and potassium. Dark buckwheat flour offers the most magnesium—more than is found in wheat, potatoes, corn and rice. It is also the best source of rutin (one of the bioflavinoids, which plays an important role in the health of the capillary system). Buckwheat is relatively non-fattening and is lower in calories than wheat, corn or rice.

Buckwheat is cheaper than most other grains because it is so easy to grow. It requires little fertilizer and is almost immune to disease. Because it is so hardy it is rarely sprayed with pesticides or herbicides.

You are probably acquainted with buckwheat pancake flour. The unmilled grain is the main constituent of kasha which nourishes millions in Eurasia. Buckwheat groats (the whole grain with the hulls removed) can be served as a hot breakfast cereal.

The recent demand for buckwheat is exceeding the supply. Grain distributors are running low and are looking for new sources.

Some distributors, like Erewhon Trading Company (Boston and Los Angeles), carry both light and dark flours.

## Oatmeal

In Wales, there is a legend of a famous giant who attributed his strength to eating oatcakes and buttermilk. In the same country, we are told, there were also two blacksmiths who walked 18 miles from Bala to Dolgelley, carried their heavy tools with them, shod about 25 horses each, and walked home the same day. As you surely do not need to be told, oats are staple fare in this part of the world, even today. More oats are used in the breakfast cereal business than any other cereal. The part that we eat is called the groat and is obtained by removing the tough hulls of the oat grains.

Interestingly enough, when oats are milled, the germ and bran remain in the portion used for human food. So actually, oatmeal is a whole grain cereal like brown rice, and contains far more nutritional value than white flour or white rice. However, the manufacturers may partially steam the oats to reduce cooking time for the consumer. The more cooking, the greater the vitamin destruction.

For maximum nutrition choose steel-cut oats. If you are looking for shorter cooking time and will settle for slightly less food value, purchase an oat cereal that specifies only five minutes cooking time. Avoid the "Quick Cooking" oatmeals that require less than five minutes to cook.

## Bulgur

What rice is to the Orient and kasha is to Russia, bulgur is to the Middle East. This is a cracked wheat that retains the bran and germ of the grain.

The Middle Easterners prepare bulgur by boiling it for one to one-and-a-half hours and then drying it in the sun. The resultant product is said to store well and be resistant to insect attacks.

Modern technology has somewhat improved the Middle Eastern process. Bulgur is processed by soaking the wheat, pressure-cooking it and drying it. Surprisingly, this manner of processing does not destroy appreciable amounts of nutrients. Bulgur is a most versatile food and easy to prepare. It tastes like rice but is much lighter and less starchy. It may be prepared like rice but takes less time to cook.

In addition to these grains and their cereals, many natural food companies offer mixed grain cereals. The Erewhon Trading Company, for example, packages mixed cereals with such fanciful names as "Mountain Gruel," "Indian Meal," "Stirabout," and simply "Breakfast Cereal," among others.

## Dispelling a Myth—Hot Cereals

Don't think that just because a cereal is served hot, it's necessarily good for you. Formerly, it was recommended that cereal be cooked two or three hours to change the starch into dextrin, a process which normally takes place when starch is digested. Later studies showed that starch is completely digested even when heated to temperatures far below the boiling point. Cooking cereals a long time or at high temperatures decreases the health-building quality of protein and causes partial destruction of the B vitamins.

No matter which selections you make, the same basic cooking principle, perhaps with a slight variation, will apply. Some prefer their porridge thin, while others like it cooked to a heavy mass. Adjust the cereal liquid ratio according to your preference. For a thicker gruel, decrease liquid by one-fourth cup or cook longer. Cereal that is too thick can always be thinned at the table with milk. Add one-fourth teaspoon salt (optional) to water and bring to boil. Slowly sprinkle in cereal so that water never stops boiling. Cook, stirring just enough to keep from sticking to the pot; too much stirring makes cereal gummy. For a richer food, use milk to replace all or part of the water.

For a creamier cereal, combine with liquid first; stir to a smooth paste; then bring entire mixture to boil and continue as above. This method is particularly good with fine-grained cereals like corn meal and rice cream, which have a tendency to stick together and form lumps. Until needed, cooked grain can be held in a covered pot off the heat. This will keep it hot and allow further drying.

## Cooking Chart

| For 1 Serving | Water | Cereal | Cooking Time |
| --- | --- | --- | --- |
| Corn Meal | 1 cup | ¼ cup | 15 minutes |
| Oats | | | |
|   Steel Cut | 1 cup | ⅓ cup | 35-45 minutes |
|   Oatmeal | 1 cup | ½ cup | 5 minutes |
| Cracked Millet | 1 cup | ⅓ cup | 7-10 minutes |
| Bulgur | ⅔ cup | ⅓ cup | 15 minutes |
| Buckwheat Groats | 1 cup | ½ cup | 15 minutes |
| Barley | 1 cup | ½ cup | 30 minutes |
| Wheat Cereals | 1 cup | ⅓ cup | 5 minutes |
| Rye | 1 cup | ½ cup | 5 minutes |
| Rice Cream | 1 cup | 3 tbsp. | 15 minutes |

Never reheat cereals. Additional heating causes a loss of more B vitamins. Try to prepare only the amount of cereal which will be eaten at one time. The practice of cooking cereal in the evening and reheating it for breakfast may save you time, but it will cost you nutrients.

# Wheat Germ: The Best Cereal of Them All

Of all cereals, wheat germ contributes the most to health. It is the very heart of the wheat kernel—the part of the wheat which sprouts and grows when planted. This part is richest in protein and thiamin, the vitamin needed to regulate carbohydrate metabolism, good appetite, growth and normal functioning of the nervous system. Iron, riboflavin, niacin, carbohydrates and fats are also present in the germ.

Farmers, with their innate wisdom, knew the value of wheat germ long before the scientists got around to acknowledging it. For instance, the farmers recognized vitamin E as a fertility factor in animal breeding. They called it freshly ground wheat instead of vitamin E, and they fed it to their stallions. They also fed it to their sows before farrowing, to promote large litters of vigorous pigs. Poultrymen insisted that fresh wheat in the diet of their chickens was essential to high egg production.

Wheat germ, of course, is loaded with wheat germ oil. When you *enrich* your family's diet with wheat germ you are giving them vitamin E (which improves endurance) plus many other vitamins, minerals, enzymes and *pacifarins,* all of which give abundant life to the growing plant—you and your family.

You get high-grade protein in wheat germ, 25.2 grams in every cup, according to the *Heinz Handbook of Nutrition*. That's more protein than you get in four ounces of turkey or two eggs, more than in a four-ounce lamb chop, a three-ounce porterhouse steak or a four-ounce hamburger.

Besides protein, wheat germ contains many important enzymes, every known B vitamin—and perhaps a few that have not yet been discovered—and practically all of the essential minerals.

Though the wheat embryo containing the germ is only a small fleck of the berry, it is, in essence, a highly concentrated form of many life-giving elements.

Since wheat germ sustains life, it invites invasion from life-seeking creatures. It contains much vitamin E which combines easily with oxygen and thus becomes rancid. This action destroys the vitamin E in the wheat germ itself, and also destroys the vitamin E already in your body. So keep wheat germ in the refrigerator, and use it quickly to benefit from all its values. If you have a large quantity, freeze most of it and use as needed.

Wheat germ may be used raw or lightly toasted and can be eaten alone or sprinkled on top of cereal, fruit or yogurt. Most people prefer the taste of the toasted germ. Raw wheat germ, however, has more vitamins because some of the sensitive B vitamins are destroyed by heat. But the raw kind is perishable. If you buy raw wheat germ and don't like the taste of it, you can spread it out in a large pan and toast it in a very low oven. This way you will lose little vitamin content.

Most cereals tend to de deficient in two of the essential amino acids—lysine and isoleucine. For a cereal to be considered a good source of high quality protein, these two amino acids, both necessary for the body to build protein, must somehow be supplied. Conveniently enough, dairy products are among the best sources of these two amino acids. The milk we add to breakfast cereal not only enhances the flavor of the cereal, but nutritional content as well. And "dairy" needn't mean milk; you'll find that cold cereals blended with yogurt, have a fresh, deliciously tangy taste.

Wheat germ is well endowed with these two amino acids. By sprinkling in one to two tablespoons of wheat germ (raw or toasted), you can add crunchiness to the texture of a cereal dish while you increase its protein value. Anytime wheat germ does not appear on the list of ingredients in a store-bought cereal, be sure to add some at the table.

Brewer's yeast is another fine way to enrich your cereals naturally. This dried yeast powder contains all the essential amino acids and is particularly strong in leucine and isoleucine. It abounds in all the B vitamins. Stir two teaspoons of the yeast, more if you like the taste, into each serving of cooked cereal.

There are also many other ways of varying breakfast cereals to increase their nutritional value and to make them more delectable. Try some of these suggestions:

\*Sweeten cereal with honey, pure maple syrup or date sugar.

*Flavor your cereals with chopped, dried fruits or raisins. No additional sweetening is needed.

*Slice fresh fruits into the cereal. Bananas, peaches and berries are as welcome on hot cereal as they are on cold. Fresh figs, orange sections and sliced pears make offbeat variations.

*Add crunch to the cereal with sunflower seeds, chopped walnuts, almonds, pecans or other nuts.

*Serve hot cereals with a pat of butter. Fat takes more time to digest than carbohydrate or protein, and so your breakfast will keep you going longer.

*Stir a tablespoon of peanut butter, soy sauce, or sesame salt into non-sweet cereals.

*Use applesauce and fresh fruit juice in the cold cereal bowl for those who cannot tolerate milk products.

## Buckwheat Delight

Here's a breakfast dish that's festive enough to double as dessert.

½ cup buckwheat groats
2½ cups boiling water
honey, to taste
raisins
chopped dates
½ cup chopped coconut

Add buckwheat groats to boiling water. Sweeten to taste with honey and add raisins and chopped dates. Boil for about 12 minutes. When almost finished, stir in shredded coconut.

This is delicious served hot or cold. Yield: 4 servings.

## Baked Breakfast Rice

Full of nutrients and a nice change in the morning menu.

2 cups cooked brown rice
1 cup raisins
1½ cups milk
honey, to taste

Mix all ingredients. Pour into deep casserole dish. Cover. Bake for 45 minutes at 325° F. Serve hot with honey and additional milk. Yield: 4 servings.

## High Protein Cereal

In a nut grinder, grind the following seeds in the proportions suggested below:

4 parts sunflower seeds
2 parts pumpkin seeds
2 parts roasted soybeans
2 parts unblanched almonds
1 part carob powder

Mix thoroughly and store in refrigerator. Serve with fruit juice, milk or fruit: bananas, berries, prunes, etc.

## No-Sugar Cereal

The night before, put the following to soak in cold water:

½ cup chopped sunflower seeds
½ cup large rolled oats
½ cup millet
½ cup buckwheat groats
1 cup unsprayed, unsulphured raisins or dried prunes

Natural Cereals from Whole Grains

In the morning, put the cereal (adding more water if needed) on a moderate heat and bring to a boil. Serve with milk. It needs no sweetener; the fruit takes care of that. Yield: 4 servings.

Below are some of the reliable mail-order companies from which you can obtain natural foods:

Arrowhead Mills (Maple Nut Granola)
Box 866
Hereford, Texas 79045

Harmony Foods, Incorporated (Harmony Grits and Mt. Kilamanjaro)
Box 1191
Santa Cruz, California 95060

Erewhon Trading Company (Maple Granola)
33 Farnworth Street
Boston, Massachusetts 02210

Honey Wheat Food Products Company, Incorporated
Richboro, Pennsylvania 18954

Lassen Foods (Granola, Honey Almond Crunch)
201 Myers Street
Chico, California 95926

Sovex, Incorporated (Crunchy Granola)
Collegedale, Tennessee 37315

Shiloh Farms (Honey Oat Crunch Cereal)
Sulphur Springs, Arkansas 72728

Walnut Acres (Sunburst Breakfast, Crunchy Cereal)
Penns Creek, Pennsylvania 17862

Below are distributors and growers that are worth seeking. Their foods are high quality, whole foods grown and processed without the use of chemicals.

Grains: Arrowhead Mills (Hereford, Texas), Erewhon Trading Company, (Boston and Los Angeles), Essene (Philadelphia), Shiloh Farms (Sulphur Springs, Arkansas), Walnut Acres (Penns Creek, Pennsylvania). Available in health food stores and natural food cooperatives; also by mail order.

Raisins and dried fruits: Erewhon Trading Company and Essene (pears, raisins, prunes, apples), Walnut Acres (bananas, apples, dates, figs, peaches, pears, prunes, raisins), Covalda Date Company, (P.O. Box 908, Highway 86, Coachella, California 92236. Will ship), Sunray Orchards (Myrtle Creek, Oregon 97457. Will ship), Ahler's Organic Date and Grapefruit Garden (P.O. Box 726, Mecca, California 92254).

Nuts: Pavone Ranch (Route 4, Box 472-A, Escondido, California 92025. Direct to consumer and through stores), Bonzana Realty (2071 Riggs Road, Lakeport, California 95453. Direct to consumer), Ehlen Citrus (20976 Road 254, Strathmore, California 93267. Sells walnuts direct to consumer).

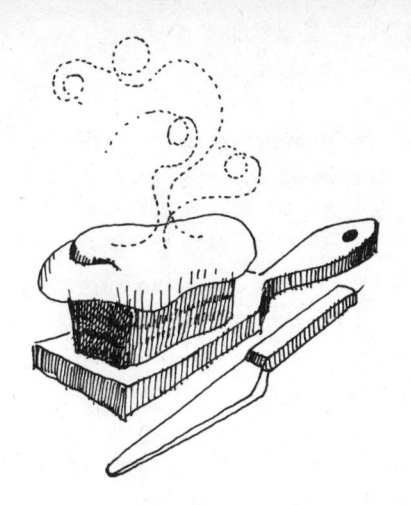

# The Art of Making Bread

Just as major breakfast foods manufacturers inflate the nutritional merits of their products in their advertising, bread manufacturers run promotional campaigns to convince us that their products will improve our diets. And like most of the processed cereals, most store-bought breads offer little nourishment.

Bread used to be called the staff of life—and with good reason. In earlier days, grain was ground between millstones which revolved slowly and stayed cool. The low temperatures kept the flour from heating, so no heat-sensitive nutrients were lost. The stones crushed the grain but did not remove any part of it. Most people then ate a whole-grain bread. White flour was available, but the cost was prohibitive for all but the wealthy.

In the mid-19th century a new refining process was discovered. This new process removed the dark, coarse parts inexpensively, but heated the flour during the procedure. The price of white flour fell sharply, and so did its nutritional content because large amounts of vitamins and minerals were either lost with the coarse parts or lost through the high temperatures.

Over the years people demanded a "purer" white flour. The milling process became more involved, and a greater portion of the grain was discarded.

The first part of the grain to go was the protein-rich bran, the outer coating of the grain. Of the many nutrients it contains, it is especially rich in iron essential for good red blood, and in phosphorous valuable for nerves and bones.

Next the germ, the very heart of the wheat, was eliminated. The germ contains a high percentage of protein, important minerals and vitamins, natural sugars, and a considerable quantity of wheat oil. These parts make up only 12 percent of the total weight of the grain, but if they are removed, nearly all the valuable nutrients in the grain go with them.

Any food value that might be left after milling is depleted still more in the bleaching that makes the flour "pure white." Next the flour is run through a bath of chemicals to preserve, age and sterilize it. Then it goes to the baker where it is conditioned, puffed up, and kept "fresh" by the addition of synthetic mold inhibitors and more preservatives.

## The Enrichment Myth

Well, what about enriched flour? Don't the bread people fortify their flours with vitamins and minerals to compensate for the nutrition-poor flour they use? Yes and no. The 33 nutrients in the wheat germ are sacrificed in making white flour. In the so-called "enrichment" process, only three of these nutrients are put back and in only one-third of the original amount.

During the forties when the original enrichment program began, Dr. W. H. Sebrell of the United states Public Health Service stated, "To me it does seem a little ridiculous to make a natural foodstuff in which the vitamins and minerals have been placed by nature, submit this foodstuff to a refining process which removed them and then add them back to the refined product at an increased cost. If this is the object, why not follow the cheaper, more sensible, and nutritionally desirable procedure of simply using the unrefined, or at most, slightly refined natural food?"

In 1970, Dr. Roger J. Williams (University of Texas, Austin) experimentally fed the kind of "enriched" bread consumed by most Americans to rats and concluded that: "Today's bread has about the same nutritional value as sawdust." Our modern "enriched" bread has been termed "pre-sliced absorbant cotton, cotton fluff wrapped in skin, pappy, tasteless, soft aerated substance that is as appetizing as white rubber without the spring and bounce."

It is preferred by the food industry because it keeps on the shelf longer than wholewheat bread and because insects avoid it—It doesn't have enough food value to keep them alive.

# The Art of Bread-Making

Baking bread has a history of long centuries behind it. The remains of Swiss lake-dwellers of

10,000 years ago show evidence that these people baked unleavened bread. The Egyptians are credited with discovering how to ferment yeast and produce the first yeast-rising bread. Both the Egyptians and the Romans knew how to separate the bran from the flour. Interesting enough, the Romans called this bran-less flour "castratus." The gladiators and others to whom health and physical strength were essential, continued to eat whole-grain breads and porridges. During the Middle Ages, baking was a closely-regulated trade, and it was not uncommon for bakers to be hanged for producing adulterated bread.

"Food serves a threefold purpose: to bring delight to the senses of taste, smell and sight, to produce health and to provide opportunity for artistic expression." Surely Adelle Davis had bread-making in mind when she gave this definition of food. There is no other form of cooking that is as simple and basic to life and nourishment, and at the same time, is as creative and as satisfying as making bread.

Bread baking in the home is enjoying a re-awakening in our culture. We are rediscovering the glorious smells of grandmother's kitchen, and the joy and wonder in eating bread we have made ourselves.

When you bake bread, organically-grown, whole-grain flours and meals are the best kind to use. If possible, buy stone-ground flour at a local mill, packaged by a natural food store, or grind it yourself from your own grains. Remember that ground grains are perishable and should be refrigerated.

When liquids are called for in bread baking, use potato water, milk or water left over from sprout-making (water in which vegetables have been cooked). Potato water can be made from a raw, diced potato with enough liquid added to make the amount needed for your recipe. Whiz the potato and water in a blender until smooth, and use the mixture in your bread. Milk should be scalded first to kill bacteria that may interfere with yeast activity. If you're reconstituting powdered milk to use as your liquid, it is helpful to heat it slightly to dissolve all the milk powder.

Though some bread recipes (notably French or Italian breads) do not call for shortening or oil, most recipes do require some oil. For light breads, stay away from stronger tasting oils like soybean, corn and peanut. Safflower and sesame oils are light enough for all breads. If you're using non-fat dry milk, use oil in your bread dough, or put butter on the bread when you eat it. Your body needs some fat to handle the fat-soluble nutrients in the milk.

Kneading stretches the gluten in yeasted breads. It should always be done on a firm, lightly-floured surface. (Never use the same cutting board for kneading bread and cutting meat; bacteria from the meat may get into nicks and cuts on the board and contaminate your bread mix.) Keep adding more flour to the board to prevent the bread from sticking to it, but try to avoid kneading extra flour into the bread. This may result in a tough loaf. Oiling your hands before kneading helps to prevent dough from sticking to them. You can stop kneading when the dough is no longer sticky but is springy and dry-moist to the touch. You'll find that, with practice, you'll develop a rhythm and feel. Kneading will be anything but the guesswork that it is in the beginning.

Put your bread in an oiled mixing bowl (allow room for the bread to rise). Place a clean tea towel over the bowl and set it in a warm, dry place to let the dough rise. A good way to see if the dough has risen is to jab two fingers into it; if the holes remain in the dough, the loaves are ready to be cut and shaped. When the dough has risen once, shape it on a cookie sheet or place it in oiled bread pans and let it rise again before baking.

There are few hard and fast rules for baking times. If you're using a loaf pan and you want to see if your bread is done, turn it upside down; if the loaf falls out readily and sounds hollow when tapped on the bottom, it's probably done. Don't be discouraged if baking times vary from those given in a recipe. Different oven conditions and climatic conditions cause variations. The addition of certain ingredients to your bread may vary baking times, too. For example, soy flour is oil-rich and develops a thick, brown crust if the oven temperature is not lowered during baking. If you're using one-fourth cup or more of soy flour for three loaves, turn the oven temperature down to 25° F. Experience is the best teacher in judging baking time.

Try brushing the tops of your loaves with butter before you bake them. This results in a rich, buttery soft crust. A mixture of egg white and water brushed on makes a glaze and is good for a hard-crusted bread. Brushing loaves with whole milk gives a sweet, moist crust.

Now, while visions of home-baked loaves dance in your head, is the time to start baking bread. Try your hand at some of these recipes. When you've had your fill of these, check natural bread cookbooks in your library and in natural food stores.

## Natural Additives for Your Own Enriched Bread

It is entirely possible to make your own "enriched" bread. There are several natural additives you can use to boost the nutritional qualities of loaves you're putting in the oven. The amount of each nutrient added to recipes depends upon both the type of bread you are making and your own taste preferences. If you're not familiar with using these additives, start by adding the recommended amount and adjust in future recipes to suit your taste.

Kelp—source of iodine. It's estimated that 1 tsp. of kelp per day is enough to correct thyroid abnormalities. Add 1 tsp. for each average-sized loaf.

*Brewer's yeast*—source of B vitamins and highly concentrated source of complete protein. You can add 2-4 tbsp. for each average-sized loaf.

*Wheat germ*—source of vitamin E. You can replace ½ cup of flour with wheat germ for every loaf.

*Rice polish*—the outer shell of the rice grain left after polishing the rice. It is a source of thiamin. You can replace ½ cup flour with rice polish for every loaf.

*Bone meal powder*—good source of calcium. You can add 1 tsp. for every average-sized loaf.

*Soy flour*—rich in protein, minerals and vitamins, especially the B vitamins. ¾ cup soy flour can replace 1 cup of wheat flour for each loaf.

*Powdered milk*—rich in calcium. If used in nonfat form, it should be used in combination with some sort of fat like oil or butter. ½ cup can be added for each average-sized loaf.

*Peanut flour*—good source of protein, B vitamins and iron. You can replace ½ cup wheat flour with ½ cup of peanut flour for every average-sized loaf.

*Sunflower seed meal*—excellent source of vitamins, protein and trace minerals. ⅛ of each cup of flour required can be replaced with sunflower seed meal.

*Cornell formula*—for each cup unbleached flour needed for recipe, first add 1 tbsp. soy flour, 1 tbsp. nonfat dry milk powder and 1 tsp. wheat germ. Then fill up the remainder of the cup with unbleached flour.

# A Word About Yeasts

Although many recipes, even those in natural food cookbooks, call for a "package of active dry yeast," most yeasts sold in individual foil packets contain BHA as a preservative. An alternative to these yeasts is compressed yeast cakes which do not contain a preservative. Another alternative is to buy natural yeasts—in bulk from your natural food store—or by mail from a natural foods distributor (Walnut Acres, Penns Creek, Pennsylvania 17862 sells this yeast by mail).

# Mike's Millet Bread

2 cakes yeast
¼ cup warm water
2 cups milk
2 tbsp. cold-pressed oil
⅔ cup honey
1 tbsp. sea salt
3 cups millet cracked in a blender
½ cup soy flour
4-5 cups wholewheat flour

Soften the yeast in water. Scald milk; add oil, honey, and salt. Pour this mixture over cracked millet, and allow it to cool, stirring occasionally. When mixture has cooled, add the yeast, soy flour, and 3 cups of wholewheat flour. Blend well. Keep adding more flour until the dough is thick and fairly dry.

Knead on floured board. And knead. And knead. Knead for about 10 minutes until the dough seems moist and stretches without tearing. Shape the dough into a ball, place in a greased bowl, and turn over once. Cover bowl with a clean towel and set it in a warm place to allow dough to rise.

When dough has doubled in volume (in about 1½ hours) punch it down, place it on floured board, and shape it into loaves. Slice top of each loaf with a sharp knife and place in well-greased loaf pans. Or, shape into round or oblong loaves and place on a cookie sheet sprinkled generously with corn meal (Ever wonder what that grainy stuff on the bottom of loaves of French bread was? Well, it's corn meal. Corn meal keeps the bread from sticking to the baking surface). If you're baking on a cookie sheet, make sure the dough is very stiff; if it isn't it will spread all over the sheet as it rises and bakes. Cover loaves and set them in a warm place to rise for 45 minutes.

Bake in a 375° F oven for about 50 minutes. A loaf is done if it can be easily removed from the pan and if it sounds hollow when tapped on the bottom.

This recipe makes a heavy bread that's very crunchy, and the soy flour makes the crust thick. For a sweeter loaf, add more honey. Delicious when eaten with organic preserves or peanut butter. Yield: 2 average-sized loaves.

## Oatmeal Bread

> 2 tbsp. baker's yeast or 2 cakes compressed yeast
> ¼ cup warm water
> 2 cups milk
> ¼ cup honey
> 2 tbsp. unrefined oil
> 1 tbsp. salt
> 4 cups whole wheat or unbleached white flour
> 2 cups uncooked oatmeal

Dissolve yeast in warm water. Scald milk, honey, oil and salt in small pot and let cook till lukewarm. In a large bowl combine yeast and milk mixture. Add 2 cups flour; mix until smooth. Stir in oatmeal and add enough of remaining flour to make a stiff dough. Turn onto lightly floured board, and knead until dough is smooth and elastic. Put in large, oiled bowl; brush top with oil and allow dough to rise until doubled (about 1 hour).

Punch down dough; shape and place in two oiled bread pans; cover and let rise until doubled (about 45 minutes). Bake at 375° F for 1 hour.

This bread may also be shaped into ovals or rounds and placed on oiled cookie sheets instead of bread pans. Yield: 2 average-sized loaves.

# Butter and Nut and Fruit Spreads

Now that you're sold on eating whole-grain breads for breakfast instead of the cottony, white stuff, what should you spread on them, butter or margarine?

Don't fall for all the big advertising campaigns praising the merits of margarine—that it tastes, looks, feels and is better for you than the "high-priced spread." Stay with butter. Butter contains many things that our bodies need, and margarine is loaded with too many things that we don't need and some that we shouldn't have. Butter is extremely rich in vitamin A and carotene (which the body can change into vitamin A). Winter butter has about 2,000 International Units of vitamin A per pound, and summer butter from cows that have been fed fish liver oil, may contain as much as 40,000 units per pound.

Butter has been called the nation's best source of vitamin A. Doctors Fraps and Kemmerer reported in the *Texas Agriculture Experimental Bulletin,* 560, (April 20, 1938) that, unit for unit, the vitamin A in butter is three times more effective than the vitamin A in cod liver oil. Vitamin A has been added to margarine because most of the oils from which margarine is made contain none of this vitamin. But vitamin A added in the form of carotene, cannot be compared to natural vitamin A because many people's bodies lack the ability to convert carotene into vitamin A. Among those able to convert it, there is a wide variance in the percentage of carotene which is utilized.

Taken year-round, butter is a good source of vitamin D. The natural vitamin D found in a pound of butter is equal to that in 10 quarts of milk.

Butter also contains lecithin, and the phosphorous associated with this lecithin is important because it is readily utilized in this form by the body. While butter is not high in mineral content, it is rich in fat-soluble factors which must be present for proper mineral assimilation. In addition, butter is the most digestible and easily tolerated of the fats.

Basically, butter is a natural carrier of vital food factors. Butter substitutes are not. Attempts to fortify other products and make them the nutritional equal of butter are largely unsuccessful. Being a natural food, butter contains all the factors necessary for the maximum vitamin effect.

The popularity of margarine has soared since World War II. Today margarine sales are double those of butter. From the beginning, low price has been the chief attribute of margarine. Today, when you buy margarine you're still paying less than you would for butter because you are buying lower-quality food. You are getting an artificial food masquerading as butter, a food greatly inferior to butter.

Those who think that margarines are all vegetable oil spreads will be surprised to learn that under the Federal Food, Drug and Cosmetic Act as amended in November 1968, margarine can be manufactured from either single or combined ingredients obtained from:

1. Cattle, swine, sheep or goats.
2. Milk (cow's) or its products (cream, buttermilk, dry or condensed milk).
4. Finely-ground soybean (whole or hulled).

The fat portion of the emulsion must be at least 80 percent of the finished product, the remaining 20 percent may consist of water, milk products or ground soybeans. Mono- and diglycerides, suspected of being cancer inciters, are added to emulsify and stabilize the water and oil emulsion. Artificial butter flavor and odor are achieved by adding diacetyl, and two flavor protectors then included. Lecithin makes the margarine fry like butter. Two more dyes make it look like butter; yellow AB and yellow OB, both made from a chemical whose safety is questioned by many doctors. Benzoates, known poisons, are then thrown in to preserve the finished product.

The current craze for margarine is based on the belief that it contains no saturated (hydrogenated) fats. This myth is hardly an accident—considering the carefully-worded advertising copy used by manufacturers. Consumer advocate, Beatrice Trum Hunter, in *Consumer Beware!* (Simon and Schuster, New York, 1971), offers fine examples of intentionally misleading advertising gimmicks:

> The advertising for corn-oil margarine states it has never been hardened by hydrogenation. While this may be true about the corn oil in the product, it fails to state that the cottonseed and soybean oils, *also present have*

Butter, Nut and Fruit Spreads

*been hydrogenated* (her italics). Another corn-oil margarine is advertised as being made from 100 percent corn oil. This may be true of the raw material used, but it fails to note that in order to make the product solid, at least part—and probably a great part— of the oil is hydrogenated. What percent is liquid? The consumer is not informed. As long as the margarine is a solid, boxed product, not flowing from a bottle, the consumer can assume that the fat has been hydrogenated.

Another artful device is to lable margarine and other factory foods as "partially hydrogenated" and "hardened" used interchangeably. These misleading phrases may be misinterpreted as a protection for the consumer. Actually, the degree of hydrogenation to which a food is subjected depends on factors of convenience for the manufacturer, packager and retailer. The consumer should remember that a product is either hydrogenated or not hydrogenated; any degree of hydrogenation is not in his best health interests.

How is liquid oil hydrogenated to become saturated, solid fat? It is first put under pressure and exposed to high temperature. Hyrogen is then bubbled through the oil in the presence of a catalyst, using nickel or platinum. During this process the hydrogen atoms combine with the oil's carbon atoms; the product becomes saturated and hardened. Technologists then bleach, filter and deodorize it and turn the original dark, greasy substance into a white, bland fat that can be further processed for making margarine.

Heating the oil ruins its original character, destroys all its vitamins and minerals and alters its proteins. Further dangers of this hydrogenation process have been described by Dr. Franklin Bicknell, consulting physician at the French Hospital, London, in his book *Chemicals in Food* (Faber and Faber, London, 1960):

> The vegetable oils are liquid oils and not solid fats because they contain higher proportion of essential fatty acids or EFA. Hydrogenation destroys the EFA or changes them into abnormal toxic fatty acids with an anti-EFA effect. . . . They accentuate in man and animals a deficiency of EFA.

So use butter. Buy grade AA butter made from sweet cream (it will be stated on the label) and not from stale cream which is made to appear fresh again by the addition of additives. Unsalted butter, although it doesn't keep as long, has fewer additives than the salted kind. If you want salt, add it at the table. To insure freshness, choose well-wrapped butter over the tub butter that is cut and weighed to order. For best keeping, store butter in a closed container in a cold part of the refrigerator, not in the butter compartment which is warmer than the main part of the refrigerator. For longer keeping, butter may be frozen.

By all means, don't limit yourself to butter as a spread on your morning bread. If you do, you'll miss out on all the fruit and nut butters, and natural jams, jellies and preserves that can enrich your bread naturally.

Peanut butter needn't be saved for sandwiches

Butter, Nut and Fruit Spreads

at lunch time. Why save all that good protein for later in the day when you really need it in the morning?

Peanut butter is easy to make at home. Grind dry roasted peanuts into a flour. If you use a mill, remove the flour from the mill and put into a bowl. Add a little oil—just enough to make the flour hold together and form a paste— and sea salt to taste. If you are using a blender, grind the peanuts in it, and while blending, add peanut oil slowly, drop by drop, until the mixture reaches the right consistency. Be careful not to add too much oil. Peanuts contains lots of oil naturally, and if an excess amount is added, the butter will become too thick and oily. When you make your own peanut butter, you can be sure that nothing has been added to it, like the hydrogenated vegetable oil (hard-to-digest saturated fat), corn syrup and dextrose found in many commercial peanut butters.

Many other kinds of nut butters can be made just as easily by grinding them. Try walnuts, almonds cashews and brazil nuts, or a combination of these. They are made in the same way as peanut butter, but may not need additional oil.

Sesame and sunflower seeds, two of the most nutrient-packed foods you can eat, can be made into meal by running them through a home mill or blender. Tahini, or sesame seed butter, can be made just as the nut butters.

Fruit butters, and combination fruit and nut butters are just as easy to make. Try some of these:

## Peach Butter

½ cup almonds
½ cup water
6 peaches, peeled and pitted
1 cup honey (optional)
1 tsp. cinnnamon

Put the nuts and water in the blender and run it until they are reduced to liquid paste. Then add the other ingredients and whiz until you have a well-blended butter. Keep covered and refrigerated.

## Pineapple Butter

2 cups pineapple chunks
2 cored apples
pineapple juice
honey to taste

In the blender, put pineapple chunks and apples, with just enough pineapple juice to blend them into a thick butter. Remove from blender and add honey. Keep in a covered dish in the refrigerator.

## Plum Butter

Pick and wash clean 1 lb. plums. Put into kettle and cover with water. Cook until tender. Put through colander to remove skins and pitts. Add honey to taste. Mix well. Cook until thick. Seal in sterilized jars.

## Seed Butter

1 cup ground sunflower seeds
¼ cup ground pumpkin seeds
¼ cup soy oil
2 tbsp. honey
Mix well, then add:
¼ cup peanut butter
¼ cup tahini (sesame seed butter)
Mix well.

## Orange Honey

Scrub the skin of an organically-grown orange, quarter it, and blend until it is fine. Add it to 3 cups of raw strained honey. Keep it in a covered can in the refrigerator between meals. This is good on waffles, pancakes and corn bread.

## Apricot Conserve

Pit and mash fresh apricots. Stir in the desired amount of honey and thicken with blanched, ground almonds. This is food for the gods, both in nutrition and taste.

## Raw Blackberry Jam

Mash ripe blackberries and add the amount of honey needed for your family's taste. Stir it in and keep the raw jam in a covered dish.

# Blueberry Jam

In the blender put the following and blend into mush:

2 cups blueberries (thawed)
1 stalk rhubarb
½ cup nuts

Pour the jam into a dish which can be covered tight. If too thin, stir in rice polishings to thicken and add honey to taste. For raw jams, comb honey is better than the liquid type. Keep refrigerated.

# Raw Marmalade

To make raw marmalade, use fresh fruits, wash and crush, or crush frozen and thawed fruits.

Any of the following fruits, either singly or in combination, can be prepared this way: peaches, plums, strawberries, raspberries, blackberries, cherries, currants.

For each cupful of fruit, use about ⅓ cup honey. (If you have honey which is crystallized, here is a good place to use it.) Thicken the marmalade with wheat germ flour, using only as much as is needed. Keep refrigerated and covered.

# Part Cooked Jam

1 cup honey
1 box pectin powder
2 cups whole, raw cranberries

Slowly boil honey and pectin powder. Add ½ cup of cranberries. Chop up remaining cranberries in the blender and add to the jell after it has boiled for a few minutes. Chill.

## Raw Pear Conserve

In the blender (or food grinder) put these ingredients:
2 cups diced pears
½ cup organically-grown unsulphured raisins
½ cup honey
½ cup nut meats
¼ cup pineapple

Blend until you have a thick jam. Put in tightly covered glass jars and refrigerate.

## Pear and Cranberry Conserve

6 ripe pears, cored
2 cups frozen cranberries
honey to taste
pinch of cinnamon and cloves

Put pears and thawed cranberries in the blender. Whiz them to a fine pulp. Add honey, cinnamon and cloves. Whiz again. Keep refrigerated in covered dish. Red raspberries may replace the cranberries. Nuts or sunflower seeds may be added.

## Pineapple Jam

½ cup cold water
2 cups fresh pineapple
honey to taste
ground nuts
sunflower seeds

Put water and pineapple in the blender and whiz until smooth. Remove from blender and add honey, then ground nuts and sunflower seeds until you have a thick jam. Keep refrigerated in a covered dish.

## Raw Strawberry Jam

Wash the desired amount of strawberries; then hull. Mash and add honey to taste. If the berries are very juicy, stir in either wheat germ flour or raw rice polishings. Add enough to thicken the jam as you want it. Tiny new mint leaves may also be shredded up in the jam for an extra-special flavor. Keep refrigerated in a covered dish.

## Tutti-Frutti Jam

Mash the following fresh fruits:

½ cup red raspberries

½ cup black raspberries

½ cup blueberries

1 ripe avocado

2 very ripe bananas

Add honey to taste, and thicken if necessary with rice polish. Add a pinch each of cinnamon and all-spice. Keep refrigerated in a covered dish.

# Corn Meal: An Early American Staple

In the untamed lands of the American Indian, corn was a vital part of the diet. The Indians had figured out every possible way to eat corn. They ate it roasted right from the stalk. They picked it green, pressed out some of the milk from the kernels and boiled the corn in the milk. They dried the mature ears and ground the kernels into meal. The Plains Indians added cornsilk to their corn meal to make it taste sweeter. The Hurons soaked young corn ears in water until they were putrid, then boiled the evil-smelling soup and drank it. Other Indians burned the corncob to ashes and mixed the ashes with their corn dishes, thereby adding minerals.

What has happened to this valuable native American food, so rich in protein, vitamins, minerals, roughage and unrefined carbohydrates? More than half the corn raised in this country is fed to animals. And much of the remainder is used to make corn starch, corn oil and distilled liquors. People still occasionally enjoy fresh ears of sweet corn in the summertime, but corn meal which sustained the Indians on long journeys and during cold winters, is hardly the important staple it was formerly.

The Natural Breakfast Book

Corn meal is so cheap that people living in modern societies feel it is "not as good" as more expensive foods such as white bread and box cakes. So tasty foods like hoe cakes, corn gems, fried mush and corn meal dumplings, which cost only a few cents, are out of place on the tables of affluent families.

An equally important reason for the dwindling popularity of ground corn is the lack of good corn from which to make first-class meal. In the time of the Pilgrims and the pioneers, corn was a primitive plant. It had been improved somewhat over its original tiny form by farmers who, over the centuries, had selected the best ears for seed. But it was still a far cry from the kind of corn we know today. The first white men to grow the plant were confronted with an early version of what we now call Indian corn. It was decorative and often very suitable for meal, but had only a moderate yield.

In the last century, plant breeders went to work on improving the corn plant. They produced sweet corn for good corn-on-the-cob eating and for general table use as a canned or dried vegetable. Moving in another direction, plant breeders selected high-yielding types of field corn for greater production of maize for cattle feed and silage. The field corn ears are big and numerous, but they aren't as good-tasting for meal nor are they as nutritional as the older, "inferior" types of corn they replaced.

Since most current seed catalogs don't offer seed for producing corn meal, some seedsmen advise the planting of Stowell's Evergreen open-pollinated sweet corn for white meal, or Country

Gentleman as a second choice, and Burpee's Golden Bantam Hybrid for yellow meal.

Most corn meal lovers think that the best corn for meal is white, because white corn has a flavor that blends with a wide variety of other foods. Actually yellow corn is richer in the precursors of vitamin A and therefore has greater nutritional value. But the flavor, texture and cooking qualities of yellow corn seem to appeal less to people who are really heavy eaters of corn meal foods.

Unfortunately, the really good meal is seldom available in the supermarkets. First, there is the question of shelf life. Whole corn that is ground into meal and stored in a warm place may "leak" some of its natural oils and stain the bags in which it is packaged. It may also attract bugs, because natural, whole corn meal is a living, vital food that appeals to insects. The scientific approach to these problems is to degerminate the meal, removing the source of the staining oil and the taste that appeals to bugs. In the process, however, the millers have also castrated the meal nutritionally and esthetically.

Inferior meal will frequently be labeled "enriched"—a backlash from the condition that existed in the South years ago when people ate almost nothing but processed corn meal and as a result got pellagra. More often than not, food enrichment is a governmental-scientific-industrial smokescreen to hide the more important fact that for some reason (usually related to profits) people are not being encouraged to eat natural, unprocessed foods.

But don't despair. There are still a few places selling good meal at very reasonable prices. Find a good source, then stick with it. (See chart in chapter on Grains)

One of the code words to look for is "bolted." A bolted meal is usually not degerminated but has had some of the larger particles filtered out through a bolting screen. Bolted corn meal is half way between processed and natural corn meal. In certain situations, a bolted meal will do until better meal comes along.

Another phrase to watch for is "water-ground." Millers who go to the trouble of keeping an old mill going under water power usually have the strength of character to use a good variety of corn to make their meal. And they generally don't go in for degerminating or enrichment. Water-ground meal is often sold in specialty food stores and sometimes even in supermarkets.

Natural food stores sometimes sell the very finest of corn meals, but this is not an inflexible rule. Buy the smallest size package of each brand and taste several before making up your mind.

Both white and yellow corn is used for stone or water-ground meal. The preference is usually regional; white is the favorite in the South, and yellow corn is more popular in other places. The way you use meal also plays a role in the color decision. Yellow seems best for muffins and mush; white a favorite for corn pones also called johnny-cakes or journeycakes.

If you're not familiar with corn meal cookery, start with these easy recipes:

Corn Meal: An Early American Staple

## Corn Meal Mush

5 cups water
1 tbsp. salt
2 cups corn meal
2 cups water

Bring to a boil 5 cups water with salt. Add corn meal mixed with 2 cups water. Cook 30 minutes or longer, stirring frequently to keep smooth. Serve with butter and either milk or syrup. Leftover mush may be poured into a deep dish that has been rinsed with water. The mush is allowed to harden and can be fried later. Yield: 6-8 servings.

## Corn Pones

Corn pones are a quickly-made substitute for bread, with a flavor and eating consistency that harkens back to pioneer days. You must have good teeth and strong jaws to eat corn pones. They quickly make you realize the sissy character of most modern foods.

1 ⅓ cups water
2 cups corn meal
1 tsp. salt
3 tbsp. unrefined corn, sesame or safflower oil or butter

Heat the water to boiling. Put corn meal and salt in a mixing bowl. Add the boiling water and oil or butter. Mix thoroughly and allow to stand covered for 15-30 minutes. Form the mixture into cakes with your hands, allowing finger ridges to remain. (Moisten your hands with oil to prevent sticking.) Bake on greased pan for 35-40 minutes in 375° F oven. Yield: 6-8 servings.

## Corn Bread

 2 packages dry yeast
 1 cup lukewarm water
 1 cup corn meal (white or yellow)
 ½ cup oat flour
 ¼ cup soy flour
 ½ cup skim milk powder
 1 tsp. salt
 2 tbsp. nutritional yeast (optional)
 3 tbsp. raw honey
 3 tbsp. oil (safflower, soy or corn)
 2 eggs, beaten

Dissolve yeast in lukewarm water and allow to stand for 10 minutes. Combine in a mixing bowl: corn meal, oat and soy flours, skim milk powder, salt and nutritional yeast, if desired.

Combine honey, oil and beaten eggs and add to dry ingredients, mixing well. Gradually add yeast mixture, blending well into other ingredients.

Pour batter into a well-oiled (9 x 9-in.) square pan. Place pan in warm area and allow corn bread to rise 30-40 minutes. Bake in preheated oven at 350° F for 30-35 minutes. Yield: 6-8 servings.

## Spoon Bread

 ½ cup skim milk powder
 1 cup cold water
 1 cup corn meal
 1½ cups boiling water
 1½ tsp. salt
 4 egg yolks
 1 tbsp. raw honey
 3 tbsp. soy flour
 2 tsp. nutritional yeast (optional)
 2 tbsp. oil (safflower, soy or corn)
 4 egg whites

Oil a 2-qt. casserole. Dissolve skim milk powder in water (using wire whisk). In medium-sized saucepan, combine corn meal and milk mixture. Gradually pour boiling water over corn meal and milk mixture, blending thoroughly. Add salt. Cook over medium heat, stirring constantly, until consistency of thick mush. Remove from heat. Let cool slightly.

Beat egg yolks until thick. Add honey. Combine soy flour, nutritional yeast and oil; add to egg mixture; mix well. Combine egg and corn meal mixture. Beat egg whites until stiff peaks form when beater is raised. Fold gently into batter and pour into prepared casserole.

Bake in preheated oven at 375° F for 35-45 minutes or until golden brown and puffy. Remove from oven and serve immediately. Yield: 8-10 servings.

# Polenta Cheese Squares

5 cups cold water
1 tsp. salt
1½ cups white or yellow corn meal
1 cup grated sharp Cheddar cheese
⅓ cup grated Parmesan cheese

Night before:

In a large, heavy saucepan, bring 5 cups cold water and salt to boil. Add the corn meal very slowly, stirring constantly with wire whisk or long wooden spoon, until mixture is thick and free from lumps. Transfer corn meal mixture to top of double boiler. Cover, and cook over boiling water for 30 minutes, stirring occasionally. Corn meal is finished when it leaves side of pan.

Remove from heat and turn corn meal mixture into a lightly oiled 9 x 9 x 2 in. shallow baking pan. Refrigerate until stiff enough to cut—allow 3-4 hours or overnight.

Morning:

Cut into 16 squares. Arrange in an oiled baking dish. Sprinkle with cheeses and place in a 400° F preheated oven and bake for 15 minutes or until cheese is melted and nicely browned. Serve immediately.  Yield: 6-8 servings.

Polenta may also be prepared by adding Cheddar cheese to mixture just before removing from heat. Pour into shallow baking pan; chill and cut into squares. Sprinkle with Parmesan cheese and heat in a moderately hot oven (375° F) until nicely browned.

# Hasty Pudding

1 quart skimmed milk
½ cup corn meal
3 tbsp. oil
½ cup molasses
1 tsp. salt
½ tsp. nutmeg
1 cooking apple, pared and diced

Oil a 2-qt. baking dish that has a cover. In medium saucepan, bring 1⅓ cups of milk to a boil; gradually add the corn meal, stirring constantly. Remove saucepan from heat and add the oil, molasses, salt and nutmeg. Stir in the diced apple. Mix well and add the remaining milk.

Pour the mixture into prepared baking dish, and cover. Bake in preheated oven at 250° F for 3¼ hours. Remove from oven and cool slightly before serving. Serve plain or with whipped, skimmed powdered milk. Yield: 6 servings.

# Eggs: the Most Nearly-Perfect Protein Food

The actual substance of eggs has been carefully compounded by nature to nourish an unborn chick to maturity. The proper food elements necessary to do the job—high quality protein, vitamins and minerals—are gathered conveniently in a package you can hold in your hand. Eat several eggs a day and you are treating yourself to nutritional excellence that is difficult to duplicate.

The white of an egg contains 10 percent protein, the yolk about 16 percent protein. Between them they have a better distribution of amino acids, the basic components of protein, than any other food. Not every amino acid can be used by your body. You must have all the essential amino acids in their proper proportions to furnish complete protein. Such complete protein also appears in foods from animal sources, meat and fish, for example. But eggs offer the most concentrated amount for building and maintaining body tissue.

Unlike food from other animal sources, there is no waste with eggs. You can even crush the shell and eat it; it's a good source of calcium!

The price of large eggs has averaged not more than 60 cents a dozen over the last several years.

## Eggs: The Most Nearly-Perfect Protein Food

A dozen large eggs weigh at least one-and-a-half pounds, which means that, at 60 cents a dozen, you pay only 40 cents a pound for the most nearly-perfect, naturally-occurring protein food.

Except for vitamin C, eggs contain just about everything we need nutritionally. They are a rich source of phosphorous, the trace minerals, vitamins A, E, K, and all the B vitamins. Eggs are second only to fish liver oils, as a natural source of vitamin D. Eggs are also an outstanding source of iron.

Here is the vitamin and mineral content of 100 grams of eggs—about 2 medium-sized ones:

| | |
|---|---|
| Vitamin A | 1140 International Units |
| Vitamin D | 50 units |
| Vitamin E | 3 milligrams |
| Vitamin B | |
| Thiamin | 120-150 micrograms |
| Riboflavin | 340 micrograms |
| Niacin | .1 milligram |
| Pyridoxine | 22 micrograms |
| Pantothenic acid | 800-4800 micrograms |
| Biotin | 9 micrograms |
| Calcium | 68 milligrams |
| Phosphorus | 224 milligrams |
| Iron | 2.52 milligrams |
| Copper | .23 milligrams |
| Magnesium | .03 milligrams |
| Chlorine | 106 milligrams |

And with all these nutrients, a large egg contains only 80 to 85 calories. Medium-sized eggs have 75 to 80 calories. They don't load you down with calories, but because of their fat and protein content they do give you a satisfied feeling that sticks with you.

Eggs contain plenty of cholesterol, and we tend to forget that the body needs this compound. In the wake of the scare concerning the part cholesterol might play in causing heart disease, some people omitted eggs from their diet. Some doctors even forbade their patients to eat eggs. After a decade of discussion, it has become apparent that the amount of cholesterol intake from foods has no real significance in causing heart disease.

Dr. Robert C. Atkins, a specialist in nutrition, diet, internal medicine and problems relating to heart disease, points out that most (about 75 percent) of the cholesterol circulating in our blood is not from the food we eat, but has been manufactured in our bodies. Writes Dr. Atkins, "We could cut out all cholesterol in our diet and our bodies would begin to manufacture more. . . If we were to outlaw eating eggs—wipe them out of our world —our average cholesterol level would fall significantly by 3 or 4 percent, not enough to change anything."

We have mechanisms in our bodies that keep the cholesterol level constant. The more cholesterol we eat, the less our bodies manufacture. In addition, lecithin, a natural compound, acts to keep cholesterol particles in the bloodstream in suspension. In this happy state cholesterol does not group into the large, clogging masses that can cause trouble. An egg provides the body with the necessary amount of lecithin to help process any cholesterol the egg contains.

The World Health Organization recently charted the incidence of heart disease in different parts of the world. Japan has had a 14 percent decrease in heart attack deaths in the last 15 years. During this time, not only was their intake of saturated fats and dairy products increased, but their consumption of eggs went up 300 percent. Many African tribes like the Masai and Somburo have very low blood cholesterols and fats. The Eskimos rarely had heart disease when they lived on the pure Eskimo diet which was nothing but fat. In similar studies the world over, the findings are the same: there is no consistent correlation between intake of cholesterol-containing foods and the change in rate of heart disease.

The real culprits in the cholesterol story may be over-processed and refined foods. Medical researchers have always had trouble developing atherosclerosis in animals until they began feeding these animals a diet of pizza, cereal, ice cream and candy. The test animals then began to develop the same kind of coronary arteries that plague Americans.

Dr. Atkins has treated some 8,000 patients who were victims of atherosclerosis. They were put on a special diet: restricted in carbohydrates, yet with no restriction on eggs, meat, fat or saturated fat. Sixty-three percent of his patients showed lower cholesterol levels after dieting. And 11 percent showed a tremendous drop of 100 points. The cholesterol problems in these cases vanished although Dr. Atkins told his patients to eat all the eggs they want.

People who stop eating eggs for breakfast often start eating cereals, breads, muffins, pancakes and doughnuts instead—and these refined foods, all high in carbohydrates, can do much harm.

In storing eggs, each passing day means a lessening of nutritional value as well as a change in taste and smell. There is no way to tell how long an egg has been around until we break it. When we buy them in a carton, we must trust the marking. If it's marked AA, the eggs should be of the highest quality with a clean, firm, thick shell and a yolk that will stand round and full when the egg is broken. Grade A is a step below this, but considered good quality and fine eating at a few cents cheaper. When an egg is Grade B, it is best used as an ingredient in custards, casseroles, and other mixtures.

It will be worth your while to find a farmer who sells "free-range" eggs. These eggs come from hens who are allowed to wander in a natural environment with other hens and roosters. The highly-confined atmosphere of egg factories combined with the artificial lighting (to stimulate egg laying) makes hens nervous and prone to disease. Hens are given heavy doses of medication daily to prevent disease from spreading through the cages.

Sir Bernard Greenwell described feeding tests that he made on chickens in England some years ago. "The grain from fertile soil was found to contain a satisfying power not produced by ordinary grain. But this was not all; resistance to disease markedly increased. In poultry, infantile mortality fell from over 40 percent to less than 4 percent."

The results of properly-fed and cared for hens can be seen at the Rodale Experimental Farm in Emmaus, Pa. There the hens and roosters are bright and alert. Contrast the farm's open, light and clean-smelling house with the typical factory farm where there are batteries of small cages with three or four birds crammed into each cage. The hen's mash and water—full of antibiotics, hormones, yolk coloring

## Eggs: The Most Nearly-Perfect Protein Food

material, patent medicines, and a host of other drugs—comes to them automatically. A conveyor removes their droppings; the whole place is lit artificially; the chickens are debeaked to prevent pecking; there are no roosters; there's only eating and laying eggs until production drops off; then the birds are killed and sold to be eaten. Factory farms forget that hens lay better eggs when they can act naturally.

Allowing chickens to range and to eat food that is natural for them, such as the insects and grasses in pasture, gives them the same health benefits we get from natural food. As Ehrenfried Pfeiffer of the Bio-Dynamic Association said, "In a test, organically-fed chickens were stronger, laid more eggs, and produced a more hatchable egg. In the chemically-fed group, only 35 percent of the eggs hatched. In the group where chickens were fed on feeds grown organically, hatchability was 68 percent."

While some nutritionists claim they can't find much difference between a fertile egg and an infertile one, there's evidence that fertile eggs do have something extra. Dr. Philip Norman of New York City treated asthmatics whom he described as "egg-eaters"—eating from two to six commercial eggs a day. One patient claimed that when he ate fertile eggs, his symptoms disappeared. If he resumed eating commercial eggs, they reappeared. The doctor then suggested to his other asthma patients—and a psoriasis patient as well—that they eat fertile eggs. "All patients obtained an excellent result," he said.

There's always the battle over which are better, brown eggs or white eggs. But there is no difference in quality because of eggshell color. There's not much difference either in the quality of eggs from various breeds of chickens, according to a New Jersey agricultural experiment station. Egg quality depends on the health of the hen, the purity and variety of her diet, and whether she is free from the stresses that result from being raised in a cage.

Did you know that chicken hysteria is a problem for commercial egg ranchers? According to a recent issue of *The Poultryman,* birds in confinement are susceptible to waves of hysteria akin to a cattle stampede. But the caged birds can hardly move, let alone stampede. So they flap and peck and raise a ruckus. A government scientist recommended easing the tension by putting tranquilizers in the poultry feed, a practice widely used today.

The United States Department of Agriculture looks at egg quality a little differently, and its grademarks are a relatively good indication of some quality factors. The USDA egg-grading service, for instance, has three grades: U. S. Grade AA (with special quality controls these may be marked "Fresh Fancy"), U. S. Grade A, and U. S. Grade B. Egg graders look for firmess of the white, the color and firmness of the yolk. They break an egg on a flat surface and measure the height of the whites and yolks with a micrometer. The firmer and higher the white and yolk, the better the grade. Grade B eggs, while as nutritious, tend to have runny whites and light yellow, watery yolks.

Unfortunately, the USDA's grading system takes no account of chemicals in the birds' feed, or whether the birds have access to range.

Fertile, organic eggs are found in many health and natural food shops these days, and when buying them, you'd be wise to find out who raised them. If the rancher is nearby (and he should be to insure freshness), you might want to pay him a visit. Buying directly from a rancher you know and trust is the best bet.

If the eggs from the nearby farmer are dirty because they were laid in the barnyard, don't wash them off until just before you use them. Nature protects the egg against bacteria by coating the outside of the shell. People who wash eggs to clean them before storage are actually destroying this layer of protection.

Store eggs in a cool, dry place, standing them on the small end. The refrigerator is best. Leftover whites may be stored in a tightly covered container for a week to 10 days. Store yolks in water in a covered container, refrigerated, for not more than two or three days.

# Egg Foo Yung

6 eggs
6 tbsp. water
1 tbsp. kelp powder
1 cup mung bean sprouts
1 tsp. fennel seeds
Put a heavy type skillet to heat.

Thoroughly beat together eggs, water and kelp. Then add sprouted mung beans and fennel seeds.

Cover the bottom of the skillet with cooking oil. Pour in the batter and turn the heat down. Cook about a minute, then cut in quarters and turn each section and brown on the other side. A minute of medium heat per side will just about do it if the skillet is preheated.  Yield: 4 servings.

## Baked Herb Omelet

> 6 eggs, separated
> 2 tbsp. cold water
> ½ tsp. salt
> 1 tbsp. brewer's yeast
> 1 tsp. minced chives
> ¼ tsp. marjoram
> ¼ tsp. chervil
> 2 tbsp. unrefined peanut oil

Beat yolks until lemon colored. Combine remaining ingredients except egg whites; add to yolks and mix thoroughly. Beat egg whites until stiff and fold gently into yolk mixture. Turn into oiled pie plate and bake at 350° F for 15 minutes. Serve immediately upon removal from oven.  Yield: 4 servings.

## Kidney Omelet

> bacon as desired
> 2 veal kidneys, cored and cut into small pieces
> 4 eggs
> 1 tbsp. oil

Grill the bacon. Drain and set aside, covered, on a warmed plate. Pour away all bacon fat, except for about 1 tbsp. Sauté pieces of kidney in the hot bacon fat for about 5 minutes; then set them aside. Break the eggs into a medium-sized bowl. Season to taste. Beat the eggs with a wire whisk or fork until yolk and white are just blended.

Warm a 10-in. omelet pan; coat bottom of pan with oil and heat till sizzling. Pour in the eggs. They will start setting immediately. Add the kidneys. Tipping the pan away from you, lift the partially-set eggs on the raised side and then tip the pan towards you to let the runny part move into the space you have made. When all the egg mixture except the surface has set (the surface should have the consistency of custard), the omlet is ready. Fold it in half with a spatula and roll it onto a serving platter. Garnish with strips of crisp bacon.

Variations:

Mushrooms and onions, finely chopped, can be added to the filling. Use only one kidney if you do this because an omlet should never be "bursting at the seams" with filling.

Chopped green pepper complements both kidney and eggs very nicely.

Some fresh herbs may be added to the egg mixture.

The omelet may be garnished with mushroom caps instead of bacon.  Yield: 2 servings.

## Scrambled Eggs in Asparagus

1 cup asparagus
dash of kelp
1 egg per person

Cut cup of asparagus in 1-in. lengths and simmer with kelp, until tender, probably 5 minutes.

Break in 1 egg per person, cutting through them as they simmer until you have them scrambled as you like them. Season again and serve.

## Polynesian Scrambled Eggs

For each person:
1 egg
1 tbsp. unsweetened pineapple juice or coconut milk
1 tsp. powdered soya or dry milk solids
dash of kelp
1 tsp. grated unsweetened fresh coconut
1 tsp. crushed unsweetened fresh pineapple

Scramble the eggs in the usual way by beating well, then blending in the pineapple juice or coconut milk, soya powder and kelp. Add coconut and pineapple and put in a well-oiled skillet over a medium flame, stir until of right consistency. Sprinkle each serving with sesame seeds. Serve immediately. (This recipe can be made in a double boiler for those who prefer their eggs scrambled that way.)

## Scrambled Eggs and Mushrooms

1 cup mushrooms, fresh washed
fresh, chopped chives or chopped green onions
kelp
1/4 tsp. marjoram
1/2 cup milk
4 eggs, whole

Chop chives or onion, kelp and marjoram into the mushrooms while you heat the milk. Now drop the eggs and seasoned mushroom mixture into the simmering milk and cut through the eggs with a spoon as the mixture cooks. Do this until the eggs just "set" and quickly remove from the fire. Serve very hot. Yield: 4 servings.

## Spanish Omelet

4 eggs
1 cup fresh mushrooms
1 small onion
½ red bell pepper
½ green bell pepper
1 tsp. kelp added last

Beat the eggs very light; then add remaining ingredients, chopped fine.

Heat a large iron-type skillet (brushed with oil) medium hot. Pour in the mixture. Brown the bottom, turn and reduce heat until browned on other side. Cut in portions and serve hot. Yield: 4 servings.

## Swiss Eggs

6 eggs
¼ tsp. salt
1 small onion
1 cup tomatoes (home canned)
1 tbsp. oil

Beat eggs and salt together until mixed. Cook onion and tomatoes with oil, then add eggs; cook slowly and stir. Yield: 4 servings.

# Sunflower Seed Omelet

4 eggs beaten very light
1 cup sunflower seed meal
½ tsp. kelp
½ tsp. caraway seeds

Heat a heavy skillet. Blend ingredients. Oil the hot skillet. Pour in the mixture; let brown on bottom, cut in quarters; turn and brown on the other side. Yield: 2-4 servings.

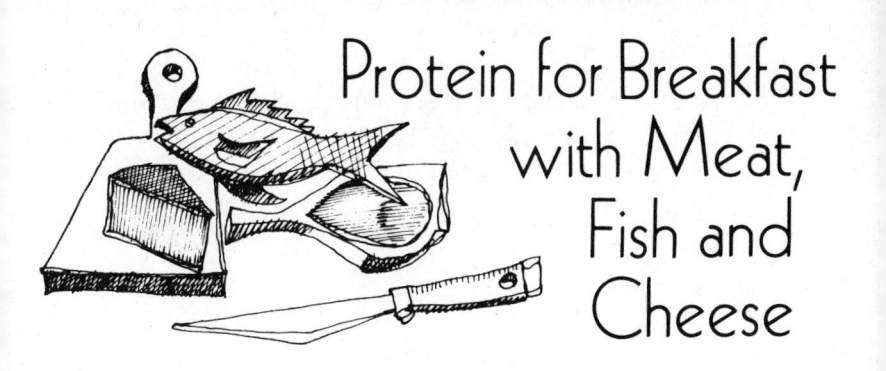

# Protein for Breakfast with Meat, Fish and Cheese

It's a well accepted fact that a breakfast containing a large amount of high-quality protein is the best kind of breakfast you can eat. In a 1943 study at Harvard University Medical School, three types of breakfast meals, each supplying the same number of calories, were served to volunteers. The high-carbohydrate breakfast consisted of a glass of orange juice, corn flakes with sugar and milk, a slice of buttered toast with jelly. The high-fat breakfast consisted of corn flakes with rich cream. The meal high in protein consisted of skim milk, lean meat and cheese. Hunger, weakness and fatigue were experienced within two hours after the high-carbohydrate meal and increased during the next two hours. After the high-fat meal, blood sugar rose quickly but fell slowly; no hunger was experienced until after four-and-one-half hours later. After the high-protein meal, blood sugar rose slowly, maintained a normal level, and no hunger was experienced until six hours later.

There are many good breakfast foods that can supply you with the high amount of protein you should have in the morning. Whole grain breads and cereals contain protein; so do butter and milk.

And, of course, eggs are an excellent source of protein. Meat, fish and cheese are good high-protein foods that are meals in themselves and can also supplement breakfasts consisting primarily of grains or eggs.

# Meat

For traditionalists, a breakfast of eggs isn't complete without a few strips of bacon, a couple of sausage links or some fried ham. Eating bacon, ham or sausage in the morning is certainly better than eating nothing, but there are drawbacks to eating cured and smoked foods. In the curing process, pork is treated with a heavy salt brine, not so much to preserve it, but to give it flavor. The saltpeter used in this brine contains nitrite, a suspected carcinogen. Some natural food stores now carry Shiloh Farms sausage links and cooked beef sausage roll, neither of which contains any nitrates or nitrites.

After treatment with the salt brine, the meat may be smoked for added flavor, with a wood such as hickory. Again, carcinogenic compounds may be produced during this smoking process. If you have a meat grinder you can make your own sausage patties from pork and beef scraps.

If you cut down on cured and smoked products, there are other meats available for breakfast. Organ meats, including liver, kidneys, hearts, brains and sweetbreads (thymus) make great breakfast foods. In addition to being rich in protein, they are the meats richest in minerals, vitamins and nucleic acids. Use them sautéed or creamed as stuffing for omelets. Of course, steak is a breakfast favorite, and combined with scrambled eggs and grilled tomatoes, steak makes a real breakfast feast.

The Pennsylvania Dutch are famous for their Pann Haas or scrapple. Alone or with syrup, this food served at breakfast, is generally made from pork scraps, ground organ meats and corn meal. But there are many variations of this food which is sliced and fried much like ham and sausage meat. If you live in the Pennsylvania Dutch area, you'll be able to buy scrapple from a country butcher. If not, try one—or both—of the scrapple recipes below.

# Pork Scrapple

5 lb. pork bones
1½ qt. water
1 bay leaf
6 peppercorns
1 lb. meat (beef, pork or organ meat)
2 cups corn meal
1 tbsp. wheat germ
1 tsp. salt
1 tsp. thyme

Put bones, water, bay leaf and peppercorns into a large, heavy pot and boil slowly for 1 hour. Add meat cut into small chunks. Boil until the meat falls from the bones, about 2½ hours. Remove meat from pork bones and chop fine with meat chunks in meat grinder, home blender or by hand. Put broth in double boiler, and when boiling, slowly add corn meal and wheat germ. Cover and steam for 30 minutes, stirring occasionally. Remove from heat when mixture is very thick and begins to leave sides of pot. Add ground meat and season with salt and thyme. Place in bread loaf pan and refrigerate at least 4 hours. When cold, it may be taken out of pan and sliced for frying. Yield: 1 average-sized loaf.

## Chicken Scrapple

2 cups corn meal
1 cup wheat germ
3½ cups chicken or turkey broth
1 tsp. chopped onion
1 cup chopped celery
2 tbsp. chopped green pepper
1 cup canned tomatoes
2 cups cooked chicken or turkey
salt and pepper to taste

Mix corn meal and wheat germ with broth and cook in top of double boiler until mixture is thick, about 30 minutes. Add onion and cook 10 minutes. Mixture should be very thick and begin to pull from sides of pot. Add salt, pepper, celery, green pepper, tomatoes and chicken or turkey. Put in loaf pan or oblong dish and refrigerate for at least 4 hours. When cold, remove from pan, slice and fry. Yield: 1 large-sized loaf.

# Creamed Sweetbreads with Mushrooms

3 pairs sweetbreads (2 lb.)
6 tbsp. lemon juice
1 small onion, peeled and sliced
1 stalk celery with leaves
2 tsp. salt
1 lb. fresh mushrooms, sliced
4½ tbsp. peanut, corn or soy oil
½ cup skim milk powder
1 cup reserved liquid from cooked sweetbreads
2 tbsp. cornstarch
3 tbsp. soy flour
¼ tsp. paprika
1½ cups chicken stock
2 egg yolks
2 tbsp. dry sherry (optional)
chopped parsley for garnish

Thoroughly wash the sweetbreads in cold running water. Place in a large bowl and cover with fresh cold water. Add 4 tbsp. lemon juice and soak the sweetbreads for 45 minutes. Drain the sweetbreads and remove the connective tissue and membrane. Place the sweetbreads in a large, heavy saucepan. Add enough cold water to cover. Add the sliced onion, cut celery stalk with leaves, 2 tbsp. lemon juice and 1½ tsp. sea salt. Place saucepan over medium heat and bring to a boil. Reduce heat and simmer uncovered for 15 minutes. Remove from heat. Using a slotted spoon, remove sweetbreads from liquid. Strain broth and reserve for sauce. Immediately plunge sweetbreads into ice water for 5 minutes. Drain, and remove any remaining connective tissue. Cut sweetbreads into cubes. Place in a bowl, cover, and refrigerate while preparing the sauce.

In a small skillet, saute the sliced mushrooms in 2 tbsp. oil, over medium heat, for 5 minutes. Set aside. In a small bowl combine the powdered skim milk with 1 cup of the reserved sweetbread liquid. Blend with a wire whisk until mixture is smooth and free from lumps; reserve for sauce.

In a heavy medium-sized saucepan, add 2½ tbsp. oil. Stir in cornstarch, soy flour, paprika and remaining ½ tsp. of salt; blend together. Place saucepan over medium heat and cook until mixture bubbles. Remove saucepan from heat. Gradually blend in the sweetbread liquid-powdered milk combination and chicken stock until mixture appears smooth. Return saucepan to medium heat and cook, stirring constantly, until the sauce is thickened and smooth. Remove from heat.

In a small bowl, beat egg yolks; spoon in a little of the hot sauce and blend together. Turn mixture into hot sauce and blend. stirring constantly. Return to heat and add dry sherry and sautéed mushrooms. Add cubed sweetbreads and simmer until thoroughly heated—Do not boil. Pour over brown rice or whole grain toast and garnish with parsley. Yield: 8-10 servings.

Protein for Breakfast with Meat, Fish and Cheese

# Organ Meat Shish Kebab

1 lb. veal kidneys
1 lb. chicken livers
1 lb. cubed veal
cherry tomatoes
mushroom caps
cubed green pepper
1 medium onion, sliced, or several small onions
seasoning to taste

Skewer all ingredients, alternating them on skewers. Brush with oil and lemon juice. Grill for about 20 minutes, turning often. Yield: 8-10 servings.

# Hash

1½ cups cooked meat (roast beef, ham, chicken or turkey)
½ cup raw, cubed potatoes (cleaned, but with skins on)
1 medium-sized onion
salt and pepper

Grind all ingredients in meat grinder or blender. Brown one large or several small patties in oiled skillet. Cook for about 30 minutes until browned on both sides. Eat plain or garnish with fried or poached egg. Yield: 2-3 servings.

# Fish

Beef is expensive to buy because it is expensive to raise. According to Frances Moore Lappé in *Diet for a Small Planet* (Ballantine Books, New York, 1971), a cow must be fed 21 pounds of protein in the form of grains to produce one pound of protein for human consumption. Economically and ecologically speaking, this is a pretty inefficient ratio. Almost 90 percent of the feed given to beef cattle is wasted because it is used to maintain the animal's body temperature. The story is the same for pork. The harvest of protein food in the form of meat is small in return for the investment of corn, grain and hay. An acre of cereals can produce five times more protein than an acre devoted to meat production, so it's understandable that meat costs so much more per pound than grain.

Fish is an excellent inexpensive source of protein and is nutritious in other ways as well. No one has to plant fish or worry over the proper proportion of elements in their diet. The incurred costs result primarily from manpower, transportation and storage expenses. Fish is chiefly protein, and its protein is as good as the protein found in beef because it supplies all the essential amino acids.

Fish are loaded with phosphorous—200 milligrams in every four ounces. In *Fish As Food* edited by Georg Borgstrom (Academic Press), we are told that certain whole fish in a normal portion of 100 grams, can supply an adult with his daily calcium need of 800 milligrams.

Borgstrom says that the iron from fish is rapidly absorbed and is especially valuable for regenerating hemoglobin in anemia cases. Fish provides a rich source of natural iodine, and thereby, an avenue for thyroid health. The thyroxine produced by the thyroid gland, works to insure proper growth, proper use of carbohydrates, physical and mental vigor, quick reactions and proper heart action. You can't get through puberty, pregnancy or lactation without a good iodine supply. In England, fish offers more than a third of the iodine consumed by working class families, even though the families eat an average of only one-half pound per week.

Fish would be doing plenty for you even if copper were its only asset. It offers a good supply (yet never too much) of this trace mineral which we need to effectively use vitamin C and to make hemoglobin out of iron. Copper is so essential in hemoglobin production that when iron fails as a treatment for anemia, a copper shortage is presumed to be the cause.

Important as these and other trace minerals in fish may be, fish liver oils contribute even more to human nutrition. They contain indispensable vitamins A and D plus substantial amounts of normally scarce vitamin E—as much as 26 to 30 milligrams per 100 grams. This means improved action in the circulatory system and muscles and more energy and endurance.

Artificial flavorings and colorings cannot be implanted in fish and ocean fish cannot be doped or injected with growth hormones.

One prominent trace mineral researcher, Dr. Henry Schroeder, director of the Trace Elements Laboratory at Dartmouth Medical School, reports that the fish to be scrupulously avoided are those taken from inland waters known to be polluted by toxic mercury dumping. Methyl mercury is indeed dangerous, says Schroeder, but the ocean is unlikely to be a major source of mercury pollution. Even if the mercury is only a minor threat, it is one more source of stress for the body.

The best way to avoid methyl mercury in fish is to pass up large predatory fish, like swordfish and tuna, which eat smaller fish and may accumulate large amounts of mercury through the food chain. Choose the smaller ones (mackerel and flounder); better yet, stay with those species that don't feed on other fish (sardines and herring). Also avoid inland fish from lakes and streams that may be heavily polluted.

Mercury pollution isn't the only reason to avoid freshwater fish. Inland fish are constantly subjected to tons of other poisons that are dumped each day into our rivers and streams by industrial firms. Unless the freshwater fish come from a mountain stream or lake that is remote enough to insure no contamination, don't eat them.

In the future, uncontaminated freshwater fish and ocean fish will be more readily available thanks to fish farming—raising fish as one would raise any other livestock. Salmon, carp, catfish and trout are just some of the fish being cultured. Until these fish are available stick with seawater fish, particularly those gathered off the coasts of Iceland, northern Canada and other remote and relatively unpolluted waters that make up the great fishing banks.

# Freezing–Best Method for Preserving Fish

For a long time there has been a prejudice in the American mind against eating commercially frozen fish, says Morris B. Jacobs in his book *Food and Food Products* (Interscience Publishers, New

York City). This is apparently because, in the early days, only those fish that seemed too far gone to be marketed, were frozen. Of course, their quality was very low. But today with the quick freezing methods that are available, frozen fish is every bit as good, or perhaps even better, than fresh fish. The marketing of fish is a race against time; the whole metabolic system of fish is set up on a very rapid scale because of the cold temperature in which they live. So deterioration sets in much faster than it does in meat. Actually the meat of a fish begins to deteriorate the moment it is taken from the water. Quick freezing halts this process immediately.

So if you live far inland, the frozen fish, packed in airtight containers very shortly after the fish is caught, has probably more food value than a whole fresh fish which has been frozen or packed in ice for the long trip from the ocean to your market. You cannot determine, says Jacobs, by the brightness of the eye or the color of the gills how fresh a fish actually is. Your only criterion for judging is the keeping quality of the fish after you buy it, its appearance and odor while you are preparing it and its palatability. Small pieces like fillets freeze more quickly than whole fish, so less food value is lost in freezing. In addition, when you buy frozen fillets there is no waste. The waste matter in a whole fish may be as high as 70 percent, as they are sold. Any housewife who has ever struggled to prepare a trout or bass brought in by her ever-loving provider knows well what a pile of fish trimmings accumulates in the garbage can compared to the tiny morsels that find their way to the table. So it's economical to buy frozen fillets.

Be wary when you purchase fresh fish. Much of it is actually frozen fish that has been thawed. Some supermarkets, like Giant in Washington, D. C., have relabeled their "fresh" fish to read more accurately, "previously frozen, thawed fish." Antibiotics, which can double the keeping qualities of fish, may be put into a dip or into the ice that surrounds fish during transportation. The fish may indeed keep longer, but to the dismay of many unsuspecting people who buy fish so treated, its strong medicinal taste destroys the delicate fish flavor. Don't learn about the antibiotic the hard way; ask the man behind the counter if antibiotics are used.

When most people think of fish for breakfast they have in mind a just-caught trout frying in bacon over an open fire. Trout is ideal for breakfast, but there are many alternatives—bluefish, salmon, lox, to name a few.

*The Complete Fish Cookbook* (Bobbs-Merrill Company, Incorporated, 1972) suggests over 500 ways to cook fish, but obviously all these variations, especially the ones loaded with garlic, wine and strong spices, aren't intended for early morning eating. Breakfast fish can be dipped in milk and cornmeal and pan-fried, or patted with butter and placed under the broiler. The can be baked in a cream sauce, poached, or steamed in fish, chicken broth or lemon water. Because fish is quick, simple to prepare and can be cooked even when fully frozen, it's a convenient breakfast food as well as a delicious change of pace.

## Salmon and Sprouts Omelet

10 eggs
1 cup bean sprouts
½ tsp. salt
2 tbsp. soy sauce
½ cup corn meal
¾ cup wheat germ
½ cup salmon

Beat the eggs and add the rest of the ingredients. Drop enough onto a moderately hot griddle to make an omelet about 4 in. across and sauté slowly, being careful not to overheat and toughen the protein in the eggs. Yield: 4-6 servings.

## Broiled Fish Fillets

½ cup corn meal
1 tsp. each kelp and fennel seeds
1 lb. fish fillets

In a bowl combine corn meal, kelp and seeds. Dip the fillets in the corn meal mixture on both sides and arrange in an oiled shallow baking pan or on the broiler rack. Put them at least 6 in. from the broiler so that they brown slowly, and bake them at least 10 minutes on each side. Garnish with finely cut parsley. Yield: 4 servings.

## Eggs Foo Yung (With Fish)

8 eggs
2 cups cooked fillet of fish, flaked
½ cup chopped green onions
1 tsp. pure honey
2 tsp. soy sauce
salt to taste
3 tbsp. safflower oil

Beat eggs slightly and add remaining ingredients except the oil. Mix until blended. Heat oil in a large skillet and drop mixture by tablespoonfuls in the hot oil. Brown on each side and serve hot with homemade applesauce or with unflavored yogurt. Yield: 4 servings.

## Fish-Corn Meal Balls

1 cup fish, cooked, flaked
2 cups corn meal mush, cooked
1 egg
1 tbsp. oil
1 tbsp. soy flour
1 tbsp. dulse, minced
2 tbsp. brewer's yeast
½ tsp. celery seeds, ground
3 tbsp. chives, minced
1 tsp. salt
wheat germ

Combine all ingredients except wheat germ and mold into balls. Roll in wheat germ. Drop into simmering fish stock or soup. Cover. Simmer for 10 minutes. Yield: 6 servings.

# Cheese

If you've got five minutes to gobble down some food and get out of the house to catch that train, bus or car ride, don't reach for a piece of bread or a muffin. Grab a piece of cheese instead. You don't have to toast it or butter it or spread it with jelly. It's quick, easy, and will get you a lot further than would a baked goodie. And if you have time to sit down and enjoy breakfast, whip up a cheese omelet or make yourself a toasted cheese sandwich on whole grain bread. Cheese is varied and versatile, and an excellent, inexpensive way of getting good protein into that first meal of the day.

The origin of cheese-making is lost in antiquity. Legend has it that an Arabian merchant, preparing for a long journey, poured some milk into his canteen, which was made from a dried sheep's stomach. He traveled through the heat of the day, then paused in the evening to partake of the food he had brought with him. To his amazement, only a thin, watery liquid came from the canteen. On cutting open the canteen, he found a mass of white curd. Thus was produced the world's first cheese. Actually, the ancient Asiatic traveler had witnessed a simple natural phenomenon—the rennin in the dried sheep's stomach had produced curds and whey from the milk placed in the canteen.

The Pilgrims brought cheese with them when they came to America. Until 1850 the art of cheese-making was largely carried on in the home. In 1851 Jesse Williams started the first cheese factory in Rome, New York. By 1870 hundreds of cheese factories had sprung up throughout the state. The industry rapidly moved westward, and now cheese-making is carried on throughout the U.S., with Wisconsin being the most important producer.

Cheese is a concentrated source of many of the nutrients of milk. It is made by the coagulation of the major milk protein, casein, and then its separation into two substances, curd and whey. Curd is a gel containing most of the protein, butterfat and a portion of the minerals from milk. Whey is mainly water containing most of the milk sugar, minerals and small quantities of protein and butterfat.

Here is what we find in *one ounce* of a variety of cheeses:

| Per Ounce | Cheddar | Cottage (from Skim Milk) | Roquefort | Swiss |
|---|---|---|---|---|
| Water % | 36 | 79 | 40 | 39 |
| Calories | 115 | 25 | 105 | 105 |
| Protein Gm. | 7 | 5 | 6 | 7 |
| Fat Gm. | 9 | trace | 9 | 8 |
| Carbohydrate Gm. | 1 | 1 | trace | 1 |
| Calcium Mg. | 221 | 26 | 122 | 271 |
| Iron Mg. | .3 | .1 | .2 | .3 |
| Thiamine Mg. | .01 | .01 | .01 | .01 |
| Riboflavin Mg. | .15 | .08 | .17 | .06 |
| Vitamin A I.U. | 380 | trace | 350 | 320 |

Basically, there are two kinds of cheeses, natural and processed. Most of the solid, hard cheeses (Muenster, Swiss, Cheddar, Edam, etc.) are natural (unless labeled "processed"), while those that are spreadable, contain fruit, vegetables or pieces of meat, flavorings or spices, are processed cheeses. Processed cheese is a blend of natural cheeses, pasteurized and mixed with emulsifiers and "optional ingredients" to form a homogenized mass. They are then aged artificially with heat and aerated to increase the volume. They are excellent examples

Protein for Breakfast with Meat, Fish and Cheese

of turning good, natural food into highly synthesized food products containing far too many chemicals and too few nutrients. If you wonder what things are considered "optional ingredients," read the label of a flavored cheese spread or a processed cheese loaf that is popularly used to make grilled cheese sandwiches.

The aging process is a vital part of cheesemaking, for it allows the moisture to evaporate and the natural oils of the cheese to develop in taste and aroma. Unfortunately, many American companies eliminate the long aging process by force-aging their cheeses with heat. Imported cheeses are usually more expensive than domestic cheeses because European cheesemakers take the time to mature their products naturally, for two months to over a year.

Genuine natural cheeses are made from certified raw cow's or goat's milk. You won't find these cheeses in the dairy counter of a supermarket, but you will see them in natural food stores and in some cheese shops. The purest, most natural cheese is made from the certified raw milk of organically-raised cows and goats. Chemical sprays and fertilizers are not used around the dairy where the milk is produced. The dairy animals are fed organically-raised feeds that are free from antibiotics and harmones. The environment is natural; the animals are encouraged to graze in chemically-free pastures. No synthetic ingredients go into the milk or cheeses, and the milk is never heated to temperatures greater than 120°F to insure that minimal amounts of vitamins are lost in the cheese making process. This organic, certified raw milk cheese is becoming more popular in natural food stores, and one company

(Wisconsin River Valley Cheese, Incorporated, R.R.5., Merrill, WI 54452) takes mail orders for their cheddar-type cheese.

All cheeses should be kept refrigerated in their original wraps. If you buy cheese cut from a bulk round and it is wrapped for you in paper, the cheese should be rewrapped in foil or plastic to keep it from drying out. Strong cheeses should be stored in a nonporus paper or a tightly-closing container so that their aromas don't leak out. Cheese may be frozen, but freezing affects the body and texture; the cheese could become crumbly and mealy. When cheese is unfrozen it should be stored in the refrigerator and used as soon as possible. Never refreeze cheese.

## Welsh Rarebit

2 tbsp. corn oil
1½ cups Cheddar cheese, diced
¼ tsp. salt
¼ tsp. dry mustard
dash of cayenne
1 tsp. Tamari soy sauce
¾ cup skim milk powder
2 cups water
2 egg yolks, beaten

Place oil in top of double boiler. Stir in and melt Cheddar cheese. Add salt, mustard, cayenne and soy sauce. Combine (with wire whisk) skim milk powder and water. Add slowly to mixture, stirring constantly. When mixture is hot (but not boiling) remove from heat. Add a little of hot mixture to beaten egg yolks; mix well. Gradually pour yolk mixture into the hot sauce, blending well. Return to low heat for several minutes, stirring constantly. Remove from heat and serve immediately on hot crackers or toast. Yield: 6 servings.

## Cheese Soufflé

4 large eggs
½ lb. Cheddar cheese
3 tbsp. oil (safflower, corn or soy)
3 tbsp. cornstarch
3 tbsp. soy flour
½ tsp. salt
¼ tsp. dry mustard
⅛ tsp. cayenne
¼ cup skim milk powder
1 cup water

Preheat oven to 350° F. Remove eggs from refrigerator and allow to remain at room temperature for at least ½ hour before using. Separate eggs. Put whites in large bowl and yolks in medium-sized bowl. Beat egg yolks well; set aside. Shred Cheddar cheese onto a piece of wax paper for easy handling and set aside.

Add oil to heavy, medium-sized saucepan. Stir in cornstarch, soy flour, salt, mustard and cayenne. Combine skim milk powder and water and add slowly, stirring constantly to keep mixture smooth and free from lumps. Place saucepan over medium heat; cook, stirring constantly until the sauce thickens and bubbles. (It should be quite thick.) Reduce heat and add Cheddar cheese; continue to stir until cheese is melted. Remove cheese sauce from heat.

Gradually pour cheese mixture into beaten yolks, stirring until well blended. Set aside to cool while beating egg whites.

Using electric mixer, set at high speed, beat egg whites until stiff peaks form when the beater is lifted out slowly. Gently fold cheese mixture into beaten whites with rubber spatula; blending thoroughly until no trace of whites show. Turn mixture into ungreased, 1½-qt. soufflé dish or straight-sided baking dish. Place soufflé on middle rack of oven and bake for 45-50 minutes; or until soufflé is puffed and golden and firm to the touch. Remove from oven and serve immediately.  Yield: 5-6 servings.

NOTE:  Please keep in mind that a soufflé must be served immediately upon removing from the oven or it will fall. The egg whites in the soufflé make it rise, and, therefore, it is very delicate. But do not be discouraged from attempting a soufflé as it is a very simple and elegant dish.

# Sugar—Thirty-two Empty Calories per Teaspoon

"There is no physiological requirement for refined sugar; all human nutritional needs can be met in full without having to take a single spoon of white or brown or raw sugar, on its own or in any food or drink." So says John Yudkin, professor of nutrition at Queen Elizabeth College, London, one of the world's foremost authorities on sugar and its ill effects and author of the book *Sweet and Dangerous*, (Peter H. Wyden, Incorporated, New York).

Is sugar the pure food the sugar industry claims it is? Yes, it is pure; no, it is not a food. The juices of the sugar cane and sugar beet, the sources of our ordinary table sugar, are filtered, refined and purified until the end product is 100 percent sugar—pure carbohydrate. It is a sweetener and only that; it contains no vitamins and no minerals, only calories. To make it "pure," sugar is stripped of every worthwhile food element.

What about the "raw" sugar that is now appearing in our supermarkets? Surely, in its unrefined state, sugar is good for you since so few of its nutrients have been processed away. Eating "raw" sugar must be much better than eating processed sugar, right? *Wrong!* This common misconception should be cleared up so those who are trying to eat nutritiously won't pay extra for "raw" sugar, thinking it is superior to the white kind.

"Raw," Turbinado, Yellow D or Golden C sugar that we find in food stores isn't raw. Truly raw sugar, the juice that comes from the sugar cane, contains about 12 to 13 percent sugar and 3 percent extraneous matter. Few of us would want to eat raw sugar without having it somewhat purified, and what's more, we couldn't, at least not in this country. By law, the sale of truly raw sugar has been prohibited in the United States since 1948.

The "raw" sugars on market shelves are at least partially refined. Some sugar companies run these sugars through all but the final washing that is given to white sugar. These "raw" sugars are nearly as refined as the white ones. Other companies refine the sugar to complete whiteness, then put back a little of the molasses that was originally removed, giving the sugar a cruder texture and a brown color.

Advertisements tell us that sugar is all energy, fuel for the body. The net effect of eating sugar is actually a drop in energy, not a gain. Low blood sugar results from eating sugar, paradoxical as this may sound. Eating sugar elevates the sugar level for a short time, then causes it to plunge far below normal.

All natural foods contain energy-producing substances. Because it is pure carbohydrate, sugar may provide energy a few minutes sooner. But consider that other foods offer energy *and* some nutrition. Along with sugar's energy you get the opportunity for tooth decay, obesity, and diabetes.

The dangers sugar-consumption holds would

be less serious if we ate only a little of it, but the excessive amounts of sugar eaten by Americans give cause for concern. In *Sweet and Dangerous,* Dr. Yudkin states that Americans consume an average of one to two pounds of sugar every week, or as much as 100 pounds a year per person.

One hundred pounds of sugar seems like an incredible amount to eat every year. But it isn't just what we sprinkle on cereal or into coffee, nor is it only what we get in sweet foods like desserts, candies and soft drinks. There is sugar in canned vegetables, salad dressings and luncheon meats. Almost every processed food contains sugar, and breakfast and convenience foods are out in front.

# Honey – the Natural Sweetener

How can you do without all the sugar you use at breakfast? What are you going to use on your cereal, over your fruit and in your tea? The best thing would be to do without, just eliminate sweeteners entirely. But if that's too big a step for you to take, there is an alternative, and that's honey.

The use of beet sugar for sweetening was introduced in 1747. With humanity's usual broad assumption that anything new is better, we took to using sugar rather than honey for baking and cooking. The full story of the results in terms of health may never be known.

The average consumption of honey is about one-and-one-half pounds per person per year. Most of us eat that much sugar in a week.

We have heard marvelous stories of the curative powers of honey. Down through the ages, it has been used as a medicine. Pythagoras advocated a honey diet, declaring that honey brings health and long life. Charles Butler in his *History of the Bees*, written in 1623, says, "Hooni cleareth all the obstructions of the body and provoketh urine. It cutteth up and casteth out phlegmatic matter and thereby sharpens the stomach of them which by reason have little appetite. It purgeth those things which hurt the clearness of the eyes and nourisheth very much; it storeth up and preserveth natural heat and prolongeth old age." Honey has been used to treat inflammation, kidney diseases, disorders of the respiratory and digestive tract, bad complexions, liver trouble, infectious diseases, poor circulation and also has been used as an ointment for wounds.

We don't often get honey in combs these days. Most honey has been removed from the tiny geometric cells of the comb in which the bees placed it. To extract it, the tops of these cells are sliced off and the open comb is placed in a centrifuge which whirls the honey out in liquid form. This is called "extracted" honey. When the comb is crushed and the honey strained from it, we have "strained" honey.

What is the food value of honey that has led people for so many thousands of years to believe in it as a food and medicine? In modern times the answer must be given in terms of vitamins. White sugar contains no vitamins. Does honey? Indeed it does. An article in the *Journal of Nutrition* (September, 1943) described the B vitamins in honey: some of the B vitamins might be destroyed in storage over a period of years: the vitamin content of pollen is much higher than that of honey, suggesting that perhaps the vitamins in honey are contained in the small pollen grains found in it; clarifying honey reduces the vitamin content up to 35 to 50 percent of the original value. (Clarifying is a process which removes the slight cloudiness that may be present, resulting in crystal-clear, brilliant honey, that is less nourishing than the unclarified product.)

The vitamin C content of honey varies, too, both with the kind of honey and the locality from which it comes. Some researchers have found as much as 311 milligrams and as little as zero milligrams of vitamin C in 100 grams of honey. An orange weighing 100 grams contains from 25 to 50 milligrams of vitiamin C. Of course, one cannot eat 100 grams of honey as casually as one might eat an orange because of honey's concentrated sweetness.

The mineral content of honey depends largely on its color. Those dark honeys, like buckwheat, are richer in minerals than the lighter ones.

With all the food value in honey it makes sense to use it instead of sugar. Honey can be used in most recipes that call for sugar. Beatrice Trum Hunter tells us in *The Natural Foods Primer* that three-fourths cup of honey can be substituted for one cup of sugar. To make up for the added liquid that honey contains, reduce the liquid in the recipe by one-fourth cup, or add 4 tablespoons of flour for each three-fourths cup honey. Honey carmelizes at a low temperature, so set your oven at a lower temperature when baking with honey than you do when you use sugar.

There are honeys and there are honeys, so be discriminating when you shop for one. First, make sure that you reach for one that says, "uncooked and unfiltered" or "raw" on the label.

The many different shades and tastes of honey vary, depending upon the area from which they come and the type of flowers and plants from which the bees take nectar. Darker honeys have a stronger taste than light ones. Most people prefer to use buckwheat honey, one of the darkest, on toast, cereals and dark bread. Willow herb and tupelo honeys and the other light honeys are best used in lighter breads, fruits and teas where the delicate flavor would be overwhelmed by a stronger honey. Honey stores well, but if it does crystallize, merely place it in some hot water or in a slightly warm oven until it melts down.

Honey isn't the only natural sweetener you can use to replace white sugar. Date sugar, available in most natural food stores, can also be made at home by grinding up pitted, hardened dry dates in a food blender or home grain mill. Of course, date sugar tastes like dates and is used most often as a garnish for cereals and yogurt at breakfast.

# Pancakes, Waffles and French Toast Made More Nourishing

Pancakes, waffles and French toast may be a nice change from ham and eggs, now and then, but when they are made with bleached flour or white bread their nutritional value is next to nothing. However, whole grain flours, oatmeal and corn meal can make pancakes and waffles which are rich in food value. French toast made with whole wheat or oatmeal bread gives a real nutritious boost to breakfast.

Ordinary recipes can be turned into high-protein ones by adding dry milk solids, the Cornell formula (see section on natural additives in Chapter 3) or eggs, or by replacing a small portion of the regular flour with a little peanut, soy or buckwheat flour. Substituting wheat germ, whole wheat, buckwheat or oat flour for some of the white flour, or adding a tablespoon of brewer's yeast, will multiply the vitamin B and mineral content, and adding some powdered bone meal or ground millet will increase your breakfast's calcium content.

The finished products may be somewhat different in taste texture, depending upon what and how much you add to the original recipe. The heavier and stronger-tasting the replacements are, the more dramatic the difference will be. Generally, for pancakes and waffles, you can safely replace one-half of your white flour with whole wheat flour, or one-fourth of your white flour with any of the other, heavier flours. Let common sense and a little experimentation be your guides.

Of course, you can put aside your own recipes and find plenty of more nutritious ones in cookbooks that specialize in natural cookery. And you can try the recipes below.

## Corn-Apple Pancakes

    2 eggs, separated
    1 tbsp. honey
    2 tbsp. oil
    1 cup milk
    1 cup corn meal, yellow stoneground
    1 tsp. kelp
    1 cup organic apples, chopped small or grated

Beat egg whites stiff but not dry. put yolks in another bowl; stir in honey, oil and milk. Add corn meal and kelp and stir till just smooth. Add apples. Fold in egg whites carefully. Put, by the tablespoonfuls on oiled griddle or skillet. Yield: 2-3 servings.

## All-Corn Waffles

    4 eggs, separated
    2 tbsp. oil
    1½ cups milk
    2 cups sifted corn flour

Blend the 4 egg yolks with the oil; add the milk gradually, then the flour.

Beat the egg whites beyond the frothy stage but not stiff. Then mix them into the batter and beat it until it is very light, and has increased in bulk about one-third. Cook the usual way for waffles. Serve with honey or maple syrup.   Yield: 6 waffles.

## Oatmeal Pancakes

2 cups milk
2 cups fine oatmeal (oatmeal may be ground in blender or grain mill)
2 egg yolks
1 tsp. honey
½ tsp. nutmeg

Scald the milk and pour it over the oatmeal. Blend thoroughly and cool. Then add the egg yolk, honey and nutmeg.

Blend together, then add the 2 egg whites which have been beaten fluffy but not stiff. Fold them in carefully and cook the pancakes on a moderate griddle which has been oiled. Yield: 6 servings.

## Barley Pancakes

½ cup warm water
2 tbsp. baker's yeast
2 tbsp. honey
2 eggs
1 cup barley flour
1 cup milk
2 tbsp. safflower or sesame oil
1 cup raw wheat germ

Pour warm water into a mixing bowl. Add baker's yeast and honey and let rise for 30 minutes, in a warm place. Add remaining ingredients.

Mix well and cook on a moderately hot griddle until done. Spread with butter and top with honey. Delicious with soft boiled eggs.  Yield: 4 servings.

## Old-Fashioned Buckwheat Pancakes

1/2 cup powdered whey
1 cup warm water
1 package baker's yeast
1 beaten egg
2 tbsp. unrefined safflower, or sesame oil
1 tsp. salt
1/2 cup pure buckwheat flour
1/2 cup wheat germ flour

Dissolve the powdered whey in the warm water, then add the yeast and let stand for 10 minutes. Add the other ingredients, mix well, and let stand at room temperature for several hours. Cook on griddle.  Yield: 4 servings.

## Syrups

Try honey on your pancakes instead of syrup. It is both sweet and syrupy but offers a far greater food value. Honey, combined with fresh or dried fruit, preserves or fruit juice to make fruit syrups, adds food value and taste variety to your pancakes, French toast and waffles.

## Basic Recipe for Honey Syrups:

½ cup butter
1 cup honey (for tart fruit juices, like lemon, add 1 ½ cups honey)
1 qt. fruit juice (orange, cranberry, grape, apricot, apple, lemon)

Melt the butter in a double boiler. Whip in the honey. Heat the mixture until the honey dissolves completely, then add the juice. Keep heating until the syrup is of desired consistency. Yield: approximately 1 pt.

## Fresh Fruit Syrups:

2 lbs. fruit (berries, strawberries, peaches, apricots, plums, nectarines)
½ cup butter
1 cup honey

Remove pits and skins of larger fruit. Purée the fruit through strainer or in blender. Melt the butter and add puréed fruit. Add honey and dilute with a little water or juice. A ½ tsp. of cinnamon may be added to peach, apricot and nectarine syrups. If too sweet for your liking, add a little lemon juice. Yield: approximately 1 pt.

## Dried Fruit Syrup:

1 cup dried apricots, apples, prunes
1 ½ cups warm water
⅔ cup melted butter
½ cup honey

Pour water over fruit and let set overnight. Place fruit and water in blender with melted butter and honey and blend. Pour into screw-top jar and keep in refrigerator. Yield: approximately 1 qt.

# Grow "Your Own" Yogurt

Basically, yogurt is milk that has been fermented by beneficial bacteria. Yogurt sets up an efficient little factory in the intestinal tract that manufactures B vitamins for you. What's more it produces friendly bacteria that help your body to fight harmful bacteria. Accord to a report in the *Journal of Biological Chemistry*, one eight-ounce serving of yogurt has an antibiotic value equal to fourteen penicillin units.

While whole milk is difficult for some people to digest, yogurt is highly digestible. Your stomach is able to digest more than 90 percent of a serving of yogurt within an hour. Along with easily assimilated protein, yogurt contains the same minerals and vitamins that are in regular milk. In brief, yogurt is milk in digestible form.

It makes good sense to eat yogurt for breakfast. It takes less time and effort to prepare yogurt than it does to mix up instant breakfasts. Yogurt has the food value to help you begin your day properly.

Most yogurts you find in supermarkets are so loaded with refined sugars, food starches, corn syrup, gelatin, artificial flavorings, colorings and preservatives that they taste like fruity ice cream sundaes, and cost you just as much in money and calories. They bear little resemblance to real yogurt.

## "Grow Your Own" Yogurt

When you buy yogurt, get the real thing.

Better yet, make your own for the purest, freshest, sweetest-tasting yogurt you've ever had! It's easy to make at home. Unlike making other dairy products such as cheese, butter and ice cream, yogurt takes little effort or time. Once you have the milk and yogurt starter mixed, all you need to do is set it aside and wait until it makes itself.

The base of yogurt is, of course, milk. Use safe (certified) raw milk if it's available in your area, because it's the most natural, wholesome milk available and will produce the most nourishing yogurt. Rigid regulations for certified milk stipulate that the health of the dairy cows must be excellent. The permissible bacteria count is lower than that in commercial milk before pasteurization, and is very often lower than commercial milk after pasteurization. Certified milk is more nutritious than commercial milk because all the butterfat and all the natural food elements are left in it.

When you make your own yogurt, you are growing vast colonies of microscopic, friendly bacteria or "plants." The starter bacteria that you introduce into the milk may be from plain, unsweetened commercially-prepared yogurt, your own homemade yogurt, or a pure yogurt culture from a natural food store. Since there are several different ways to encourage incubation, you might like to experiment with a few methods, and then choose the way that works best for you. This will depend upon how much equipment you want to use and how much time you want to spend in yogurt- making. Whatever equipment you do use, make sure that it is scrupulously clean. Remember, you want to encourage the growth of beneficial and not harmful bacteria. An unclean bowl or spoon might give an off-taste to your finished yogurt.

Nutritionist Adelle Davis makes her yogurt in an earthenware bowl because it retains heat well. Miss Davis says to mix one quart of milk with one-fourth cup commercial yogurt. Fasten a cooking thermometer to the side of the bowl or float a dairy thermometer on the surface. Set the bowl in the oven and heat slowly to 120° F. Turn off oven, cover milk to hold in heat, and let cool gradually to 90° F. Maintain temperature between 90° to 105° F by reheating oven if needed (about 2 to 3 hours) until milk becomes the consistency of junket. Check frequently during the last 30 minutes. Chill immediately after milk thickens.

Natural foods expert Beatrice Trum Hunter prefers to use a commercial yogurt-maker or culturizer. This consists of a constant-temperature, electrically-heated base and a set of plastic or glass containers with tight-fitting lids. Culturizers make four individual pints or quarts at a time, depending upon the model. They are foolproof, cost from 10 to 15 dollars and are available at most natural food stores. Mrs. Hunter says to pour a quart of milk into a pot and bring to a near boil. Cool to lukewarm (105 to 115° F). Mix the contents of a package of Bulgarian yogurt culture into the milk with a wooden spoon. Pour the mixture into pre-warmed cups of a yogurt-maker, cover and leave undisturbed for about two hours. At the end of this time, remove the lid from one container and gently tilt the glass. The yogurt should be about the consistency of heavy cream. If it's still thin, let it incubate longer and check again. When the yogurt thickens, remove from refrigerator.

"Grow Your Own" Yogurt

There's also a way to make yogurt using no special equipment at all. It takes a little longer, but is just as easy and less expensive since you don't have to buy any thermometers or yogurt-makers.

Heat milk to almost boiling and let it cool. When the milk is lukewarm, add one-half cup yogurt for each quart of milk and stir well to make sure there are no lumps. Then warm a casserole dish—by running hot water over it or heating it for a few seconds in a very low oven. Pour the mixture in the warm dish and cover. Wrap the casserole dish in a large towel and set in a quiet, warm spot in the kitchen. Leave undisturbed for at least six hours and let it set overnight. At the end of this time, check the consistency of the yogurt by unwrapping the towel carefully and tilting gently. If it is solid enough for your liking, refrigerate immediately. Serve only when thoroughly chilled.

This method of yogurt-making is very simple, but not as foolproof as the others, since it is difficult to maintain a constant temperature in the milk mixture. The warmer the spot where the mixture sets, the quicker it will thicken and be ready, providing the area is not over 115° F. If you're not successful using this method the first time, try it again until you find just the right spot in your kitchen and until you know how long to let it set.

An extremely simple way of making yogurt is to use a thermos bottle. A thermos is an excellent heat retainer. Once the starter has been stirred into the lukewarm milk, pour it into a wide-mouthed thermos, put on the lid and let it set four to six hours before refrigerating. This is practically foolproof, since the temperature is controlled for you.

Yogurt may be made with a variety of ingredients. Any kind of milk may be used. Goat's milk is preferred by some since it is more digestible than cow's millk. For vegetarians, those allergic to regular milk, and for the adventuresome, soybean milk makes an unusual yogurt.

To make soybean milk, wash soybeans and soak them overnight in lots of water. Put one cup of soaked beans and three cups of new water in the blender and whiz until pulpy. Use up the beans in this proportion. Place this blended mixture in a large stainless steel, pyrex or porcelain pan (do not use aluminum) and simmer gently for 15 minutes. Strain through a very fine sieve or a double-thickness of cheesecloth. Refrigerate until ready to use. Use soybean milk to make your yogurt, following any of the procedures already outlined.

All yogurt will thicken as it cools, but if you like a thicker, richer, sweeter yogurt, add one-half cup powdered skim milk or one-and-one-half cups evaporated milk to the warm milk and starter.

Yogurt will keep well for about eight days if kept in an air-tight container. Make sure that you save some to start your next batch. The new starter should be used before it is five days old.

Yogurt-making is a simple procedure. Once you become familiar with the method you have chosen you'll be able to make perfect yogurt every time.

Properly-made yogurt should be rich and custard-like and have a creamy, slightly tart taste. Homemade yogurt will be sweeter than any store-bought variety. If, after refrigeration, there is a little water (whey) on top of the yogurt, don't worry, you haven't done anything wrong. This is natural,

## "Grow Your Own" Yogurt

especially after it has set in the refrigerator for a few days. Open a commercial yogurt and you'll find water on top, too. Either mix it in or pour it off, but save it for using instead of water in other recipes, since the whey is high in vitamin $B_{12}$ and minerals.

If you have trouble making yogurt the first time, check for the following problems:

1. Perhaps the milk mixture was disturbed while incubating. Even a few tilts or knocks can cause the whey to separate from the curd. Instead of getting a thick and smooth yogurt, it may be watery and lumpy.

2. Perhaps your mixture was too hot or too cool. If the mixture is too cool, the growth of bacteria will be retarded. If it's too hot, the bacteria may be killed. Add more starter, incubate longer and adjust temperature to correct.

3. Perhaps the milk or yogurt starter was not too fresh. The older either is, the longer it will take to incubate and the more starter you should use. For best results, neither should be more than five days old.

4. Perhaps you used a pure yogurt culture which may take longer to thicken than prepared yogurt.

Flavor your yogurt with anything that has a natural sweetness—let your imagination go wild. Add a drop of vanilla extract, or some carob powder and honey to a dish of yogurt. Try some yogurt with honey and fresh fruit, or chop up dried fruit that has softened in a little water overnight. Many commercial yogurts add preserves for flavoring and you can add your own preserves—made with honey—to your yogurt.

Try yogurt on strawberries, blueberries or sliced peaches for a special breakfast.

Here are a few yogurt recipes that are delicious for breakfast:

# Apple Delight

4 apples, washed, unpeeled
1 tbsp. fresh lemon juice
1 tbsp. raw honey
½ cup chopped dates
1 cup yogurt
chopped nuts—garnish

Core apples and shred. Blend in lemon juice, honey and dates. Fold in yogurt. Serve, topped with chopped nuts, as a dessert or salad. Yield: 4 servings.

# Fruit Yogurt Salad

1 cup yogurt
½ cup crushed drained, canned, or fresh pineapple (if canned, use the kind that comes in its own juice).
1 tbsp. honey
3 ripe sliced bananas
chopped nuts
½ cup crushed berries

Mix together yogurt, pineapple, honey and bananas. Sprinkle with nuts and crushed berries. Chill for 2 hours before serving. Yield: 4 servings.

# Fruit Juice Yogurt

Mix together 3 cups plain, unflavored yogurt with 1 cup apple, grape, orange or cranberry juice. Serve over fruit or granola. Yield: 4 cups.

# Fruits and Fruit Juices

You can't lose by adding fresh, vine-ripened fruit to your breakfast table. Fruits are among the richest sources of vitamins A, B, C, and P—and many minerals. Fruits also have an abundance of natural sugars. The sugar content in fully-ripened dates, for example, is 35 to 75 percent of their total weight. And when most fruits are eaten in their raw, whole state, few of their original vitamins are destroyed.

Commercially-grown fruits are usually heavily-sprayed crops. Most fruit farmers follow spraying programs that require several applications of insecticides every season, with heavier doses each year. Fruit growers use parathion, malathion, dieldrin (and until fairly recently, DDT) and other pesticides which are ranked with the most toxic chemicals; a taste will kill. The soil under the tree-plant becomes saturated with toxic substances and if the sap rising in the spring carries poisons with it, the fruit can be impregnated with spray materials.

The skin of the fruit contains the largest amount of this residue. While it is common to remove the skins of lemons, oranges and grapefruit, how can you peel a heavily sprayed strawberry or blueberry. You can remove the skin of an apple or peach, but you're also peeling away the part richest in minerals. The chemicals are distributed throughout the cells of the fruit and there is no way to wash them off completely.

Commercially-grown fruit may not taste the way it should because it was not left on the tree, bush or vine to ripen. It is a common practice to pick fruits while they are still unripe if they are to be shipped long distances and then ripen them artificially just before they reach the market. Bananas, papaya, grapefruit, lemons, oranges, melons, pears and persimmons may be artificially-ripened with ethylene gas. Oranges and grapefruit are usually dyed. And oranges, lemons, limes, melons, apples, pears, peaches, plums and strawberries may be waxed to deceive consumers into thinking the fruit is fresh and ripe when in fact it may have been picked several weeks earlier. These fruits cannot match naturally ripened fruits in taste or nutritional content.

Growth hormones, applied to increase the size of fruits, may make them gigantic in size, win them prizes at county fairs as well as high prices in the market place, but only at the sacrifice of flavor. Grapes can be swelled 20 to 60 percent of their normal size with the hormone, gibberellic acid, but why?—It makes them tasteless.

On the other hand, organically-grown fruits are grown by people who strive for quality, not quantity and uniformity. Organic farmers work in harmony with the cyclic patterns of nature. Contrary to chemical farmers, organic growers do not use materials and methods outside of nature's pattern. They know that by replenishing the soil every season with organic matter like composted wastes, animal manure and cover crops, and natural mineral fertilizers, they are replacing the naturally-occurring nitrogen, minerals and other soil elements that are continuously being consumed by growing crops.

Organic farmers work with the environment, not against it. Rather than use costly chemical insecticides that upset the ecology, pose dangers to human and other animal life and demand heavier applications the more they are used, organic growers utilize biological insect controls. Plant-derived insecticides that decompose readily and do not threaten the environment and beneficial insects that prey on crop pests are the organic farmer's weapons.

But where can you get organically-grown fruit? You won't find it in supermarkets very often. Farm markets do offer a wide selection of produce, and by asking clerks and farmers you should be lucky enough to find fruits that are grown organically and not doctored up with cosmetics. Natural food stores carry local produce that is grown without chemicals in the summer, and may have it shipped to them all year round from natural and organic food distributors. Ask them where they get their fruit, and if they have affidavits and test analyses of crops to insure that the fruits have never come into contact with chemicals. Look for signs that say the fruit was produced by a certified organic grower.

*Organic Gardening and Farming* magazine (Rodale Press, Emmaus, Pa.) has its own certification program, and farmers in certain states including Maine, California and Oregon, have similar programs that assure consumers of chemically-free produce.

## Fruits and Fruit Juices

You can also order directly from distributors and growers by mail. Below is a list of fruit growers who have unadulterated, chemical-free food available by mail order.

*Erewhon Trading Company,* 33 Farnsworth Street, Boston, Mass. 02210
   dried apples and pears, raisins and prunes.
*Walnut Acres,* Penns Creek, Pennsylvania 17862
   dried bananas, apples, peaches, pears, figs, dates and raisins
*Covalda Date Company,* P.O. Box 908, Highway 86, Coachella, Calif. 92236
   dates and citrus fruits
*Sunray Orchards,* Myrtle Creek, Oregon 97457
   prunes
*Ahler's Organic Date and Grapefruit Garden,* P.O. Box 726, Mecca, California 92254
   dates and grapefruit
*Patron Angel Citrus Groves,* 311 60th Street, N.W., Bradenton, Florida 33505
   oranges and grapefruit
*L.P. Dewolf,* R.F.D. #1, Box 10, Crescent City, Florida 32012
   oranges
*Lee's Fruit Company,* Box 450, Leesburg, Florida 32748
   oranges
*A.J. Broderson,* Route 2, Box 490, Merritt Island, Florida 32952
   oranges

Although it is better to eat the whole fruit or vegetable because you get the full food value of both the pulp and the juice, fresh home-squeezed fruit and vegetable juices can enrich and brighten up an ordinary breakfast. If you're lucky enough to have an organic garden, you can pick your fruits and vegetables that same morning and use them as the source for the freshest, purest juices possible.

Juicers, available in many health food stores, department stores and natural foods mail order houses are quite inexpensive, and once you make a permanent fixture in your kitchen, you'll realize how valuable they are in allowing you to get the most nutrition and variety from fruits and vegetables.

There are two basic types of juicers. The most common is comprised of a perforated metal basket that sits atop a high-speed rotary plate. The plate has hundreds of small raised cutting edges. When a carrot, for example, is forced into the hole on top of the machine, the teeth on the plate rip open the tissues and destroy the cell walls; juice and pulp are then free to go their separate ways. The high-speed whirling plate hurls the pulp and juice mixture at the walls of the basket and the juice sprays off from the centrifugal force and runs down the case into a spout where you collect it.

This is the usual type found in the home. It has to be cleaned out after each use because the basket fills up with fine, slightly-moist pulp—which is perfect for the compost pile or the chicken yard.

The second type has a screw-type cutter to rupture the cells. The juice falls by gravity, and the pulp is continuously ejected, so that you don't have to clean the machine during a day's juicing. This type is more suited to restaurants and health bars. It also costs more.

You do, of course, toss out some nutrients and food value with the pulp. So drinking juice isn't a substitute for eating fruits and vegetables. It is, however, a delicious and refreshing *adjunct* to our meals, insuring us of plentiful quantities of the essential nutrients in vegetables. And it tastes great.

Vegetable juices are raw, with almost all the vitamins, minerals and enzymes of the whole vegetable intact. Although children may balk at eating all those vegetables, they will probably love the taste of cold, fresh carrot juice and you can juice about any vegetable—beans, peas, lettuce, celery, spinach, parsley, and so on.

For something really delicious and different, try raw fennel juice. Fennel is a delightful celery-

The following chart shows the approximate nutritional contents of important juices:

| | BEET (Red) | CARROT | CELERY | CUCUMBER | Romaine LETTUCE | PARSLEY | RHUBARB | SPINACH | TOMATO | WATERCRESS | APPLE | COCONUT | GRAPE | GRAPEFRUIT | LEMON | ORANGE | PINEAPPLE | POMEGRANATE |
|---|---|---|---|---|---|---|---|---|---|---|---|---|---|---|---|---|---|---|
| PROTEIN % | 1.6 | 1.1 | 1.1 | 0.8 | 1.2 | 3.5 | 0.6 | 2.1 | 0.9 | 1.7 | 0.1 | 1.4 | 1.3 | 0.4 | 0.9 | 0.6 | 0.4 | 1.5 |
| FAT % | 0.1 | 0.4 | 0.1 | 0.2 | 0.3 | 1.0 | 0.7 | 0.3 | 0.4 | 0.2 | 12.5 | 0.1 | 0.1 | 0.6 | 0.1 | 0.3 | 1.6 |
| CARBOHYDRATE % | 9.7 | 9.3 | 3.3 | 3.1 | 3.0 | 9.0 | 3.8 | 3.2 | 4.0 | 3.3 | 12.5 | 7.0 | 19.2 | 9.8 | 8.7 | 13.0 | 9.7 | 19.5 |
| CALORIES PER PINT | 220 | 217 | 89 | 84 | 94 | 283 | 115 | 115 | 112 | 109 | 250 | 700 | 462 | 200 | 210 | 265 | 207 | 472 |
| CALCIUM % | 0.140 | 0.225 | 0.390 | 0.050 | 0.345 | 0.350 | 0.220 | 0.390 | 0.055 | 0.785 | 0.035 | 0.120 | 0.055 | 0.105 | 0.110 | 0.120 | 0.040 | 0.030 |
| MAGNESIUM % | 0.130 | 0.100 | 0.140 | 0.050 | 0.065 | 0.160 | 0.085 | 0.250 | 0.065 | 0.170 | 0.040 | 0.100 | 0.045 | 0.045 | 0.045 | 0.055 | 0.050 | 0.020 |
| POTASSIUM % | 1.770 | 1.540 | 1.460 | 0.700 | 1.660 | 1.50 | 1.625 | 2.685 | 1.335 | 1.435 | 0.640 | 1.500 | 0.530 | 0.805 | 0.615 | 0.905 | 1.350 | 1.600 |
| SODIUM % | 0.485 | 0.385 | 0.645 | 0.050 | 0.100 | 0.200 | 0.125 | 0.445 | 0.060 | 0.495 | 0.055 | 0.180 | 0.025 | 0.020 | 0.030 | 0.060 | 0.080 | 0.250 |
| PHOSPHORUS % | 0.210 | 0.205 | 0.230 | 0.105 | 0.140 | 0.130 | 0.090 | 0.230 | 0.145 | 0.230 | 0.060 | 0.370 | 0.050 | 0.100 | 0.055 | 0.070 | 0.055 | 0.050 |
| CHLORINE % | 0.290 | 0.195 | 0.665 | 0.150 | 0.395 | 0.090 | 0.180 | 0.330 | 0.145 | 0.305 | 0.025 | 0.600 | 0.010 | 0.025 | 0.030 | 0.025 | 0.255 | 0.068 |
| SULPHUR % | 0.090 | 0.110 | 0.140 | 0.155 | 0.130 | 0.120 | 0.065 | 0.180 | 0.070 | 0.835 | 0.030 | 0.140 | 0.045 | 0.050 | 0.045 | 0.050 | 0.045 | 0.040 |
| IRON % | 0.004 | 0.003 | 0.003 | 0.002 | 0.007 | 0.016 | 0.003 | 0.013 | 0.002 | 0.015 | | | 0.0015 | 0.0014 | 0.003 | 0.002 | 0.002 | 0.004 |
| SILICON % | 0.009 | 0.007 | 0.008 | | | | 0.006 | 0.020 | 0.009 | | 0.006 | | 0.002 | | | 0.0007 | | |
| MANGANESE % | 0.008 | 0.0005 | 0.0014 | 0.0013 | 0.0064 | 0.008 | 0.0013 | 0.0042 | 0.0012 | 0.0036 | 0.0003 | 0.0017 | 0.0001 | 0.0001 | 0.0002 | 0.0003 | 0.006 | |
| COPPER % | 0.001 | 0.007 | 0.001 | 0.016 | 0.0003 | 0.015 | 0.0005 | 0.001 | 0.0005 | 0.005 | 0.0008 | 0.0009 | 0.0005 | 0.0003 | | | 0.0008 | 0.0004 | 0.0005 |
| IODINE Parts per billion. | 230 | 180 | 500 | 650 | | 400 | | 350 | 180 | | | | | | | 200 | 120 | |

U.S. Dept. of Agriculture Chart

*This chart, prepared by the United States Department of Agriculture, measures percentages of various nutritive elements in vegetable juices. The bulk of juice is, of course, water. Cabbages eaten whole are 97 percent water, for instance, so by juicing them you're retaining more than 97 percent of their nutritive elements.*

like plant that has the tangy, cool flavor of anise. Fennel juice tastes sweet, with a hint of licorice.

Or try Jerusalem artichoke juice. This tuberous root is sweetened naturally with levulose, a sugar even diabetics can tolerate. And celery juice is known as a champion thirst-quencher and heat mollifier for hot-weather gardeners.

The following recipes come from Brownie's—the famous health food restaurant in New York City that started in 1936 as a vegetable juice bar. Brownie's still knows the value of these drinks and has perfected some truly delicious ones. In all these recipes, prepare the other juices first, pour them in an eight-ounce glass and fill with carrot juice.

## Honi-Lulu

2-in. wedge pineapple
juice of ½ orange
carrots
Yield: 1 serving.

Note: Citrus is better juiced in a citrus or hand juice squeezer.

## Orange Blossom

½ McIntosh apple
juice of ½ orange
carrots
Yield: 1 serving.

Fruits and Fruit Juices

## Sunshine

2-in. wedge pineapple
juice of ½ orange
dash of papaya syrup concentrate
squeeze of lime juice
carrots
Yield: 1 serving.

## Vegetable Garden

1 beet
3 leaves escarole
2 leaves chickory
1 scallion
1 radish
carrots
Yield: 1 serving.

# Herb Teas

The amount of caffeine in a cup of coffee or tea is quite small. Yet we drink cup after cup of these popular beverages and that adds up to quite a bit of caffeine consumed. Because caffeine is a stimulant it can become habit-forming. It makes you breathe faster, raises blood pressure, strengthens your pulse, stimulates your kidneys, excites functions of the brain and temporarily relieves fatigue or depression. Caffeine causes an increase of 3 to 10 percent in the basal metabolic rate (the rate at which your body makes use of the food you eat) within the first hour. Any increased energy brought on by artificial stimulation is temporary and will be followed by a reversal that drags efficiency to a point far below the norm.

Those who drink one or two cups of tea or coffee a day need not worry about cutting it out of their diets; the little caffeine they consume won't do any harm. But those who drink several cups more each day should be concerned. Since caffeine is a stimulant, people who have heart trouble or high blood pressure should avoid drinking both tea and coffee altogether.

# Herb Teas

What should you drink in place of coffee and tea? Centuries ago, when coffee and tea were unheard of or available only to the wealthy, every family had its herb garden to supply the family with a vast array of aromatic, flavorful herb teas or tisanes, as they are called. Every housewife was a specialist in the knowledge of just what herbs combined best to cure a cough, fever, rheumatism, hives or whatever ailed members of her family.

The marvelous age-old folklore that has grown up around the properties of various berries, seeds and leaves in the sickroom undoubtedly has many truths to it. There are healthful benefits from drinking herb teas. Because there are so many kinds of herbs from which to choose, there are exciting combinations that can be made. The aromas of herbal teas are exotic, and their unique and delicate flavors add an unusual touch to an ordinary breakfast.

Remember, when preparing the herb tea (tisane) that its delicate flavor can be impaired if it is not made properly. People who know their herb teas, never brew them in metal since this affects the flavor. They use only china, glass, earthenware, porcelain or enamel. Usually one level teaspoon of dried herb leaves or three teaspoons of fresh leaves is adequate. Both seeds and whole leaves should be bruised well before steeping. Lengthy steeping can ruin the flavor of any delicate herb, so it is best to steep the leaves for a short time, using more leaves if a stronger taste is desired. Authorities will suggest you drink a tisane lukewarm. Not everyone agrees. The theory is that extreme heat or cold will destroy beneficial enzymes. But those who drink tisanes for the taste, and not medicinal reasons, don't hesitate to drink it hot or even iced.

Herbs can be grown in the smallest gardens, in their own tiny plot, along borders or snuggled between flowers and vegetables. The apartment dweller or the one-room boarder can grow herbs on a windowsill.

For those whose thumbs are not tinged with green there are many places to obtain dried herbs and spices for a tisane. Herb teas can be purchased in most natural food stores and gourmet shops as tea bags and as loose tea.

The most popular drinks are the mint teas, lemon balm and chamomile. The various mints all make good teas, either from the dried or fresh leaves. Spearmint, peppermint, apple mint or wild mints make pick-me-up teas that leave a refreshing taste in the mouth. They may be sweetened with honey or flavored with lemon.

Lemon balm is made like all other herb teas. It should be allowed to steep for 10 minutes or more as it does not deteriorate from longer steeping. A very pleasant light lemon flavor and real lemon aroma make this a popular tea. It is excellent mixed with pekoe.

Drinkers of chamomile tea guarantee that it aids digestion and helps to relax fidgety people. Because chamomile flowers are so delicate, they should not be steeped more than three to five minutes.

# Convenient Breakfast Foods for Hurried Mornings

Convenience foods are popular at breakfast time because so many Americans don't have time—won't take time—to prepare and eat a full meal. While these instant breakfasts are easy enough, few come close to being nourishing breakfasts. Despite their manufacturers' claims, instant breakfasts you drink through a straw, pop out of a toaster or pour into a bowl are primarily carbohydrates jazzed up with artificial colors, flavorings, and other additives that make them appear like something they are not. Their prices are many times over the cost of the foods themselves—manufacturers charge high for their creativity, elaborate packaging and advertising campaigns.

You don't have to pay big prices and sacrifice nutrition for convenience. There are simple no-cook foods that offer high-quality nourishment, yet take less than three minutes to prepare. They are all made with natural, whole foods and cost considerably less than those mixtures that food factories create for us.

# Breakfast Sundaes

This instant breakfast is based on the make-your-own sundae idea, using plain, unflavored yogurt. To ready this meal take out your jars of assorted raw nuts, pumpkin, sunflower and sesame seeds, dried fruits, wheat germ, honey, maple syrup and molasses and place them on the table. Give everyone a bowl of yogurt and let each add his own toppings. Fresh fruit slices, when available, or homemade preserves and fruit butters made with honey may be added with, or used instead of, the other toppings.

# Fresh Fruit Shakes

For each serving:

3/4 cup water

6 tsp. dry milk powder

1-2 tbsp. honey

1 tbsp. wheat germ

fruit (1 peach, 1 orange, 1/2 banana, 1/2 cup diced cantaloupe or 1/2 cup berries)

2 ice cubes

Combine water, milk powder, honey, wheat germ and fruit of your choice in blender container. Blend at high speed until smooth, then add ice cubes, 1 at a time through feeder cap while machine is running and process until ice is liquefied. Pour into a tall glass and serve.

## Tiger's Milk

For each serving:

1/2 cup orange or pineapple juice
1/2 cup milk
1-2 tbsp. brewer's yeast powder
1 tbsp. soy or safflower oil
1 tbsp. dry milk powder
1 egg
1/2 tsp. vanilla

Combine orange or pineapple juice, milk, brewer's yeast powder, oil, dry milk powder, egg and vanilla. Shake until smooth or process in blender.

## Date-Nut Nog

For each serving:

1/2 cup almonds
3 pitted dates
3/4 cup milk or 3/4 cup water
6 tsp. dry milk powder

Grind almonds to a powder in blender container. Add dates, milk or water plus dry milk powder. Blend until smooth.

## Breakfast Banana Drink

1 pt. yogurt or buttermilk
2 large or 3 medium ripe bananas
3 tbsp. brewer's yeast
2 tbsp. lecithin
1/2 tsp. vanilla extract

Liquefy all ingredients in blender to make delicious "milk shake." For variation try adding carob powder or an egg. Yield: 2 servings.

## Rose Malone's Nut-Milk Shake

⅓ cup raw cashew nuts
1 cup water
3 ripe bananas
2 tbsp. brewer's yeast
¼ tsp. kelp

First blend nuts and water in liquefier to make milk. Then add other ingredients and blend again. Serve immediately. Yield: 2 servings.

# Breakfasts for People Who Hate Breakfasts

Some people simply don't like the usual breakfast foods—the eggs, the pancakes, the cereals. But this is no reason for skipping the meal entirely. Traditionally we associate certain foods with breakfast. If these foods don't appeal to you, eat others.

Certainly you've heard of the great English breakfasts, with sideboards heaped with beef kidneys, chicken livers, kippers and fish. The Japanese often serve soup for breakfast. Athletes eat steak at breakfast, for extra protein before a big game.

Probably the most convenient non-breakfast foods are last night's leftovers. These foods have already been prepared and need only to be heated. Last evening's casseroles and vegetables, chicken, beef or fish add variety to a breakfast. Some people are so fond of leftovers that they make extras for dinner just to make sure there will be plenty left for morning.

Almost any dinner food can double as a breakfast food. Mild soups and stews are as easy to make in double batches as they are in single ones. Try to get plenty of protein into whatever breakfast you choose—lots of meat or fish, whole grains or milk solids. Meat loaf is a good dish, if you leave out garlic and other flavorings that pack too big a wallop for the early morning. Meatless dishes, like cheese-rice casseroles, or pilaf made from bulgur, kasha or brown rice, are high in protein and these are quickly and easily reheated.

Liver, steak and fish are great foods at any time of day, and since they can be broiled or pan fried quickly, they are perfect egg and cereal substitutes.

Who says you have to serve eggs boiled, fried or scrambled for breakfast? If you don't go for eggs the usual way, serve them in a fresh, exciting style! Transform a few eggs into a fancy cheese or bacon soufflé, a quiche, an omelet or a french pancake with fresh fruit inside. Egg custard, generously covered with granola and a little milk, is a nice way to get your eggs, milk, whole grains and natural sweeteners in one delightful, easy-to-make dish.

# Cream of Carrot Soup

1 onion, diced
3 tbsp. oil (soy, safflower, or corn)
1 lb. carrots (5-6 large) unpeeled, thinly sliced
4 cups vegetable stock or water
1 cup skim milk powder
2 cups cool stock or water
salt, white pepper, to taste
chopped fresh dill or parsley for garnish

Sauté onions in oil until transparent. Lift out of pan and put into blender. In same pan, sauté carrots until tender. Set aside ⅓ of the carrots. Put

2/3 of sautéed carrots in blender. Add 1/2 cup of stock or water and purée. Heat in the top of a double boiler. Combine skim milk powder with remaining stock, using a wire whisk. Add to purée. Add salt and pepper. Add the reserved 1/3 sautéed carrots to the soup. Garnish with dill or parsley. Yield: approximately 6-8 cups.

## Soybean Vegetable Casserole

- 1 cup diced celery
- 2 cups sliced carrots
- 1 medium onion, chopped
- 1 tsp. sea salt
- 3 tbsp. peanut oil—soy or corn oil
- 1/4 tsp. rosemary
- 2 tsp. freshly chopped parsley
- 2 tsp. powdered vegetable broth
- 2 cups tomato purée
- 2 cups bean liquid or water
- 3 cups cooked soybeans.

In large skillet sauté celery, carrots and onion in oil until tender but not brown, about 10 minutes. Add seasonings and powdered vegetable broth to sautéed vegetables; slowly stir in the tomato purée and bean liquid or water. Simmer mixture for about 15 minutes. Stir in cooked soybeans and simmer about 10 minutes longer. Turn mixture into a 2-qt. ovenproof casserole and bake in a preheated oven at 350° F for 1-1 1/2 hours or until beans are tender. Remove from oven and serve immediately. Yield: 8 servings.

## Baked Soybeans

½ cup green pepper, chopped
¼ cup onions, chopped
cold pressed oil (enough to sauté vegetables in)
1 lb. soybeans, cooked (reserve cooking water)
¾ cup catsup
1½ tsp. salt
½ tsp. kelp
2 tbsp. honey (raw)
1 tbsp. molasses (dark)

Sauté green pepper and onions in oil until tender. Combine soybeans, cooking water, sautéed vegetables, catsup, salt, kelp, honey and molasses in casserole and bake 1½ hours at 350° F stirring occasionally. Yield: 8-10 servings.

## Method for Soaking and Cooking Soybeans

1. Soak soybeans in cold water to cover them until they swell. (1 hour or so)
2. Then either: a. refrigerate them overnight or for 12 hours or: b. bring them to a boil in a saucepan, boil 1 or 2 minutes, cool, freeze overnight. (The freeze method will lessen the amount of cooking time needed.)
3. Bring soybeans and their soaking water to a boil, then turn down heat and simmer until they are tender—2 or 3 hours. Add 1 tbsp. of oil per cup of beans to cooking pot, and use a large enough pot so that when they are covered with a lid, the soybeans will not boil over.

# Vegetable-Beef Loaf

1 onion, chopped
1/3 cup green pepper, chopped
1/3 cup celery, chopped
1/2 cup carrot, shredded
1 tbsp. oil (peanut, corn or safflower)
3 tbsp. soy grits
2/3 cup tomato juice
1 lb. ground beef (chuck or round)
2/3 lb. ground beef heart (if heart is not available, substitute 1/2 lb. ground beef)
2 eggs, beaten
1/4 cup skim milk powder
1/2 cup raw wheat germ
3 tbsp. chopped parsley
2 tbsp. catsup
1/3 tsp. sea salt
1/3 tsp. pepper
1/3 tsp. thyme
1/3 tsp. basil

Sauté onion, green pepper, celery and carrot in oil. Soak soy grits in tomato juice for 5 minutes. Combine meat, eggs, skim milk powder, wheat germ, parsley, catsup and seasonings. Add sautéed vegetables mixture and the soy grits-tomato mixture. Mix well.

Oil 9x5x5-in. loaf pan, bottom and sides, and press meat mixture into pan. Bake in a preheated oven at 350° F for 1 1/4 hours or until meat at center is cooked. Turn out of loaf pan, slice and serve. Yield: 6-8 servings.

## Honey Egg Custard

2 cups milk, scalded
1/3 cup honey
1/8 tsp. salt
3 eggs
1 tsp. vanilla

Blend all the ingredients well by hand or in food blender. Pour in individual custard cups or in casserole dish. Place the dish or cups in a pan of hot water. The water in the pan should be about 1 in. deep. Bake in a slow oven (300-350° F) for 1 hour or more. Custard is done when knife inserted into center of custard comes out clean. Serve warm or cooled with granola and milk.  Yield: 4 servings.

## Fruit Filled French Pancakes

2 tbsp. wheat germ
3/4 cup unbleached white flour
1/2 tsp. salt
1 tbsp. honey
2 eggs
2/3 cup milk
1/3 cup water
1/2 tsp. vanilla
1 tbsp. butter or sesame or safflower oil
2 cups sliced apples, bananas, peaches, apricots or berries

Run wheat germ through food blender until finely ground. Sift together the flour and salt. Add to wheat germ in mixing bowl. Mix together the honey, eggs, milk, water and vanilla, and combine them with a few quick strokes to the dry ingredients. Ignore the lumps.

Heat a skillet and add butter or oil. Pour in some batter (pancakes should spread thin) and sprinkle with your choice of fruit. Cover with more batter. Turn when bottom is browned. Serve with honey or fruit syrup. Yield: 10 medium-sized pancakes.

# Breakfasts Are a Must, Diet or No Diet

If you are skipping breakfast to lose weight, stop! You are defeating your purpose. You are running the motors of your metabolic machinery at low speed. What you want to do to burn fat, is shift into high. You can do this best when you enjoy a breakfast that contains at least one-fourth of your day's protein requirements—usually about 22 grams.

Those who omit breakfast not only accentuate their hunger, but also suffer a significant loss of efficiency in the morning hours, invite the devastating effects of low blood sugar and slow down their metabolism—a condition which leads to low energy and extra pounds.

To diet successfully, you should do exactly the opposite of saving calories. Invest your calories wisely, especially for breakfast. You will reap dividends in terms of increased energy, vitality and an over-all sense of well-being.

Haggard and Greenberg of Harvard in a study of the relation of diet to efficiency (*Journal of the American Dietetic Association*, XV, 1939, 485) found that when people failed to eat breakfast, their blood sugar dropped slowly but continuously throughout the morning. They worked slowly, made many mistakes and suffered from fatigue; they became more inefficient as the morning wore on. Although lunch gave them a pick-up, their blood sugar soon fell way down again.

This is the syndrome you invite when you fail to eat a proper breakfast. The ironic part is that while you suffer these manifestations of hunger in the interest of losing weight, you are actually not helping your body to burn up excess poundage at all.

Dieters have actually gained weight during the period they went without breakfast or only drank coffee and they have lost weight when they were eating high calorie breakfasts.

Where the big breakfast really helps is during that period after supper when some people have an overpowering urge to eat high-calorie snacks. You eat that extra food in the evening not because your body needs it, but because your mind is unsettled as the result of a wrong eating pattern throughout the day. When you start the day without breakfast, or with just a cup of coffee and a sweet roll, you look forward to making up that deficit in food later, usually at the evening meal. But the trouble is that by concentrating your big eating toward evening, your mind continues in the direction of food even after supper, and you need a bedtime snack too. With that pattern, you go to bed with a full stomach and that food goes to make body fat because you don't have an opportunity to burn it off.

To *want* to eat breakfast—and to get the big benefits of protein food in the morning—you have to stand back and look at the day as a 24-hour thing.

Think of *when* you are going to want to be the most active, *when* you need the fuel and energy of a good meal, *when* your body is going to be in the best condition to do the work of digestion. After looking at the day in perspective, you'll probably see that the daylight hours are the time you need the most energy, and therefore, eating a good meal *before* starting your day's activities is the most sensible thing to do.

Dr. Harvey Smith, a specialist in treating obesity, believes that 90 percent of American fatties could lose weight by reversing the order of their daily meals: eat breakfast at dinner time and dinner in the morning.

This theory makes a lot of sense. The calories for meals eaten early in the morning are burned off by the day's activities. Calories consumed in the evening at dinner time have less chance to be utilized and frequently turn into fat. Dr. Smith believes that eating habits should be rearranged so that as many as 80 percent of the day's calories are contained in breakfast and lunch, leaving just 20 percent for dinner time. This is one way you can enjoy all the calories your body needs, suffer no hunger pangs, and trim your figure at the same time.

Now you've told yourself that you should eat breakfasts—that you must eat breakfasts to get the most energy from food and still lose weight. You've sold yourself on that most important meal of the day, but you find it difficult to eat a substantial breakfast because you're not hungry enough. If this is the case, chances are you ate too much the night before.

Start eating less for dinner. Try cutting out

dessert after dinner and forget midnight snacks. Eat a smaller portion of everything. Hunger sets in only when the blood sugar drops to about 70 milligrams; the blood sugar level is usually 95 milligrams after the typical American dinner, so you can eat less and still not get hunger pangs a couple of hours later. Try a late afternoon snack—raw nuts or sunflower seeds—to take the edge off your appetite for the evening meal and help you cut down on dinner calories.

Try some exercise before breakfast to increase your morning appetite. This is a good time for your jog around the block or for your daily push-ups. Soon you will find that your meal schedule has adjusted and your body has grown accustomed to eating large breakfasts and smaller meals later in the day.

# Index

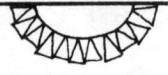

Amino acids, 22, 58
Apple delight, 110
Apricot conserve, 45
Atkins, Robert C., 60-61

Baked breakfast rice, 24
Banana drink, 125
Barley, 15, 100
BHT-BHA preservatives, 8
Bicknell, Franklin, 42
Blackberry jam, raw, 45
Blueberry jam, 46
Bone meal powder, in bread-
    making, 33
Borgstrom, Georg, 78
Bread
  corn, 54
  enriched, 33-34
  millet, 35-36
  natural additives for, 33-34
  oatmeal, 36-37
  spoon, 54-55
  whole wheat, 29
Bread-making, art of, 27-37
Breakfast
  dieting and, 134-135
    need for, 134-137
Breakfast cereals, 5-7
Breakfast rice, baked, 24

Breakfast sundaes, 124
Brewer's yeast, 22, 33
Brown rice, 13-14
Buckwheat, 15-16, 101
Buckwheat delight, 23
Bulgur, 17-18
Butler, Charles, 94
Butter, nutritional value of,
    38-39
Butter spreads, 38-48

Carotene, 39
Carrot soup, cream of, 128
Cereals
  cooking chart for, 19
  high protein, 24
  no-sugar, 24-25
  sweetening of, 22-23
Cheese
  for breakfast, 85-88
  types of, 86-87
Cheese soufflé, 89-90
Chicken scrapple, 74
Choate, Robert B., 6
Cholesterol level, 60-61
Convenience foods, 123-126
Corn-apple pancakes, 99
Cornell formula, in bread-
    making, 34

# Index

Corn flakes, 5-6
Corn meal, 49-57
Corn meal mush, 53
Corn pones, 53
Corn waffles, 99-100
Cranberry preserve, 47
Cream of brown rice, 14
Cream of wheat, 8

Date-nut nog, 125
Dieting, breakfast and, 134-135

Egg foo yung, 65-66, 84
Eggs
   nutritional value of, 58-70
   Polynesian scrambled, 68
   salmon and sprouts omelet, 83
   scrambled with asparagus, 67-68
   scrambled with mushrooms, 68-69
   Swiss, 69
Erewhon Trading Co., 10, 16, 18

Fats, saturated, 40-41
Fish, for breakfast, 77-80
Fish-corn-meal balls, 84
Fish fillets, boiled, 83
Flour, white vs. whole wheat, 27-29
French toast, 98-103
Fruits and fruit juices, 112-119
Fruit shakes, 124

Granolas, 9-10
Greenwell, Sir Bernard, 62

Groats, 15
Gussow, Joan, 7

Hash, 77
Hasty pudding, 56-57
Herb omelet, 66
Herb teas, 120-122
High-protein cereal, 24
Honey, 94-97
Honey egg custard, 132
Honi-lulu, 118
Hot cereals, myth of, 18-19
Hunter, Beatrice Trum, 40, 106

Jacobs, Morris B., 80
Jacobson, Michael J., 7

Kasha, 15
Kelp, in bread-making, 33
Kidney omelet, 66-67

Lappé, Frances Moore, 77-78
Lecithin, 39

Mail-order companies, natural foods and, 25
Margarine, vs. butter, 39-41
Margolius, Sidney, 9
Marmalade, raw, 46
Meat, for breakfast, 72-73
Mercury pollution, 79-80
Merrill, Annabel L., 10
Mike's millet bread, 35-36
Milk, in bread-making, 34
Millet, 14-15, 35-36

Natural cereals, from whole grains, 5-26

# Index

Natural foods
   distributors and growers of, 26
   mail-order company suppliers, 25
   retail stores for, 3
Norman, Philip, 63
No-sugar cereal, 24-25
Nut and fruit spreads, 38-48
Nut-milk shake, Rose Malone's, 126

Oatmeal, 8, 17, 100
Oatmeal bread, 36-37
Oils, hydrogenation of, 41-42
Orange blossom, 118
Orange honey, 45
Organically grown food, 2-3, 113-115
Organ meat shish kebab, 77

Pancakes, 98-103
   French, 132-133
Pann Haas, 73
Peach butter, 44
Peanut butter, 42-43
Peanut flour, 34
Pear conserve, raw, 47
Pfeiffer, Ehrenfried, 63
Pineapple butter, 44
Pineapple jam, 47
Plum butter, 44
Polenta cheese squares, 55-56
Pork scrapple, 73
Protein, 20-21, 71-72

Rice, 13-14, 24
Rolled oats, 11

Salmon and sprouts omelet, 83

Schroeder, Henry, 79
Sebrell, W. H., 29
Seed butter, 45
Sesame seeds, 43
Soybeans, 129-130
Soy flour, 34
Spanish omelet, 69
Spoon bread, 54-55
Strawberry jam, raw, 48
Sugar, 91-93
Sunflower seeds, 34, 43, 70
Sweetbreads, with mushrooms, 75-76
Swiss muesli, 9-10
Syrups, 101-103

Tiger's milk, 125
Tutti-frutti jam, 48

U.S. Public Health Service, 29

Vegetable-beef loaf, 131
Vitamins, 20-21, 38-39, 59, 112

Waffles, 98-103
Watt, Bernice K., 10
Welsh rarebit, 88-89
Wheat germ, 20-23, 33
Whole grains, natural cereals from, 5-26
Williams, Jesse, 85
Williams, Roger J., 29

Yeast, in bread-making, 30-31, 34
   brewer's, 22, 33
Yeast powder, 22
Yogurt, 104-111
Yudkin, John, 91